PRAISE FOR *THE BIG BOOK OF JOB DESCRIPTIONS FOR MINISTRY*

The Big Book of Job Descriptions for Ministry is an outstanding resource to help churches and church leaders clarify ministry positions and to motivate members to greater ministry. I recommend this manual to all church leaders who desire to be good stewards of the gifted people in their churches.

Dr. Thom S. Rainer
Dean, The Southern Baptist
 Theological Seminary
President, The Rainer Group
 Church Consulting

Finally! A resource worth its weight in gold to the local church! Larry Gilbert and Cindy Spear have given us a remarkable time-saving tool with which to lead and organize our volunteers! As a pastor I only wish I had a tool like this 20 years ago. The hours I spent writing just such descriptions of ministry could have been spent in far more productive ways. The accompanying CD enabling every pastor, regardless of the size of the church, to quickly and easily adapt the descriptions to his/her church is invaluable. This one's a WINNER!

David Slamp
Pastor of Adult Ministries
Central Community Church,
Wichita, KS

After having examined *The Big Book of Job Descriptions for Ministry*, I found myself thinking, *This manual fills one of the greatest vacuums in church ministry today*. Larry and Cindy's written job descriptions are the most needed tools for churches that have been developed in many years. It covers all of the ministry jobs that can be imagined. It will circumvent multitudes of potential misunderstandings about responsibilities of paid staff and the vast army of lay volunteers. This is a must for every pastor who wants to improve the performance of the church staff and volunteers, and at the same time keep them happy in their ministry.

Lindsay Terry, Ph.D.
Author

The *Big Book of Job Descriptions for Ministry* will be a blessing to every church office. I highly recommend this book for any pastor who really wants to define ministry team roles in the local church.

Dr. Stan Toler
Author/Speaker
Oklahoma City, OK

There are a vast number of churches that do not have ministry job descriptions for the tasks that they ask people to do. Is it any wonder that many people are not effective in ministry? *The Big Book of Job Descriptions for Ministry* helps solve that problem. This manual includes job descriptions for not only paid staff, but also for the vast number of positions that are filled by volunteer workers. May God use this manual to help us all become more effective in His work.

Dr. Elmer Towns
Dean, School of Religion
Liberty University

Costume Designer/Seamstress 110

Creative Dance Ministry Director 111

Creative Dancer 112

Decorations Assistant 113

Decorations Coordinator 114

Drama Director 115

Drama Team Leader 117

Drama Team Member 118

Narrator 119

Set Design/Construction Crew Leader 120

Set Design/Construction Crew Member 121

Set Painting Artist 122

Special Production Director 123

Theatrical Makeup Artist 124

Family 126

Family Life Pastor 127

Hospitality 129

Fellowship Coordinator 130

Food Service Assistant 131

Food Service Director 132

Greeter 133

Hospitality Coordinator 134

Kitchen Director 136

Parking Lot Attendant 137

Reception Server 138

Usher 139

Welcome Center Guide 140

Library 141

Book Processing Assistant 142

Book Reviewer 143

Desk Clerk 144

Historian 145

Librarian 146

Yearbook Assistant 147

Yearbook Coordinator 148

Media 149

Audio Technician 150

Lighting Technician 151

Photographer 152

Public Relations Assistant 153

Public Relations Coordinator 154
Public Relations Graphic Designer 155
Public Relations Writer 156
Sound Technician 157
Tape Ministry Director 158
Video Technician 159

Men's **160**
Men's Ministry Director 161
Men's Small-Group Leader 163

Music **164**
Children's Choir Member 165
Children's Music Assistant 166
Children's Music Director 167
Handbell Choir Director 168
Handbell Choir Member 169
Music Director 170
Music Ministry Librarian 172
Orchestra Director 173
Orchestra Member 174
Organist 175
Pianist 176
Praise Team Leader 177
Praise Team Member 178
Preschool Choir Member 179
Preschool Music Assistant 180
Preschool Music Director 181
Sanctuary Choir Member 182
Youth Choir Assistant 183
Youth Choir Director 184
Youth Choir Member 185
Youth Praise Band Director 186
Youth Praise Band Member 187

Nursery **188**
Nursery Caregiver 189
Nursery Coordinator 190

Outreach/Inreach **191**
Benevolence Minister 192
Bereavement Minister 193
Bread/Cookie Baker 195
Bread/Cookie Taker 196

HOW TO USE THIS RESOURCE

This resource lists many ministry positions—some of them may fit your church to a *T*, while others may lean toward a much smaller or larger church ministry. Some churches will need to combine the responsibilities of two or more positions into one—based on church size, need and budget—until time requirements and the scope of the positions grow. If you currently have other positions in your ministry or eventually develop new ministries that are not listed here, follow the same formula for writing descriptions for your own ministry. For each ministry position—from the groundskeeper to the pastor, from the part-time volunteer to the full-time paid staff member—determine and specify the following information in light of your own church's beliefs and needs.

Time requirements and duties of the positions listed in this manual will vary depending on the size and needs of your church. Also note that there is one ministry description per position; however, you may need more than one person to fill some ministry positions. For instance, you may need one children's church leader, but several children's ministry chaperones. You will be able to determine how many people you need in each position and which positions your church must fill according to your church's size, ministry emphases, goals and vision. Be sure to give each person involved in ministry—or each one considering a ministry position—a copy of the written ministry description related to his or her area of service or interest. This will help clarify expectations and insure a more efficient ministry.

Take a moment to review the following format, which is used throughout *The Big Book of Job Descriptions for Ministry* and provides an example for you to follow in developing new ministry descriptions.

SAMPLE MINISTRY DESCRIPTION FORMAT

First, state the basic function of this position in one to three sentences. For example:

> The adult class prayer leader is responsible for praying fervently, organizing and leading a class prayer chain and encouraging spiritual growth in class members through daily devotions and prayer.

Then determine the following:

Ministry Area/Department

What department or ministry area will this position come under (e.g., administration, children's, hospitality, creative arts)?

Position

What will be the title of this position? The title should reflect the age group, responsibilities and function of the position (e.g., Christian education director, preschool teacher, youth chaperone, yearbook coordinator, usher).

Accountable To

Who would the person in this position go to for direction, approval and help (e.g., pastor, Christian education director, fellowship coordinator)?

Ministry Target

What is the specific target group to whom the person in this position will minister (single parents, the church in general, young marrieds, pastor)?

Position Is

Will this position be
- ❑ Volunteer?
- ❑ Paid staff?

Some positions might begin on a volunteer basis and change to a paid one as the ministry grows.

Position May Be Filled By

- ❑ Church member
- ❑ Regular attendee
- ❑ Other approved individual (those not attending this church)

Minimum Maturity Level

- ❑ New, growing Christian
- ❑ Stable, maturing Christian
- ❑ Solid, very mature Christian—previous ministry experience preferred

Spiritual Gifts

Which spiritual gifts would best enhance the person's ability to fulfill the responsibilities of this position (e.g., administration, mercy showing, serving)?

Talents or Abilities Desired

What specific talents, abilities or experience would help the person be most effective in the position (e.g., public speaking, organizing, creativity, construction experience, social work, computer skills)?

Best Personality Characteristics

How would you describe the type of person who might best carry out the duties of the position or best relate to the ministry target (e.g., outgoing, fun loving, serious, compassionate, analytic, expresser, dependable-leader)?

Passion For

What is the type of ministry or the specific people group for whom this person should have deep concern (e.g., for teens, elderly, special needs, music, teaching)?

ADMINISTRATION

ADMINISTRATIVE ASSISTANT

The administrative assistant is responsible for providing professional administrative support for the pastoral staff and coordinating tasks with the church secretary/receptionist.

Ministry Area/Department	General staff/administration
Position	Administrative assistant
Accountable To	Pastor
Ministry Target	Pastoral staff
Position Is	Paid staff
Position May Be Filled By	Church member
Minimum Maturity Level	Stable, maturing Christian
Spiritual Gifts	Administration • Serving
Talents or Abilities Desired	Experience in secretarial and administrative tasks • Computer literate and accurate typing, 55+ wpm • Good organizational skills • Detail oriented • Pleasant phone manner
Best Personality Traits	Dependable • Discreet • Friendly • Professional • Neat
Passion For	Providing administrative support to church pastors and managing an organized and efficient church office
Length of Service Commitment	Two years minimum

ANTICIPATED TIME COMMITMENTS

1. **Doing ministry/preparing for ministry**: forty hours a week
2. **Participating in meetings/training**: up to four hours a month

RESPONSIBILITIES/DUTIES

1. Participate in staff planning meetings.
2. Compose or transcribe correspondence for pastoral staff.
3. Keep accurate church records, including attendance, membership, baptismal, marriage, newsletter, special mailing lists, etc.
4. Use desktop-publishing software to prepare:
   a. Church newsletter
   b. Special flyers as needed
   c. Bulletins
5. Make phone calls as directed by pastoral staff.
6. Order/maintain office and administrative supplies, including stamps or postage for postage meter.

7. Prepare and maintain annual reports, minutes from monthly business meetings and other special projects as directed by pastoral staff.

8. Maintain schedule of appointments for pastor(s).

9. Maintain master calendar of events.

10. Keep lists of hospitalized church members, special prayer requests, deaths, births and other important events. Mail cards from church as appropriate.

11. Oversee/delegate tasks to the administrative secretary/receptionist.

ADMINISTRATIVE SECRETARY/RECEPTIONIST

The administrative secretary/receptionist is responsible to provide clerical support to the administrative assistant and pastoral staff and to present a positive image to those who contact the church by phone or in person.

Ministry Area/Department	General staff/administration
Position	Administrative secretary/receptionist
Accountable To	Administrative assistant
Ministry Target	Pastoral staff/church in general
Position Is	Paid staff
Position May Be Filled By	Church member or regular attendee
Minimum Maturity Level	New, growing Christian
Spiritual Gifts	Administration • Serving
Talents or Abilities Desired	Clerical skills such as filing and typing • Pleasant phone manner • Computer keyboard knowledge/experience • Organizational skills
Best Personality Traits	Dependable • Discreet • Friendly • Professional • Neat
Passion For	Providing clerical support to church staff and greeting church members and the public, presenting a good Christian testimony to those who contact the church office
Length of Service Commitment	One year minimum

ANTICIPATED TIME COMMITMENTS

1. Doing ministry/preparing for ministry: twenty hours a week
2. Participating in meetings/training: up to one hour a month

RESPONSIBILITIES/DUTIES

1. Participate in staff meetings upon request.
2. Receive, screen, direct incoming calls. Take messages when appropriate and distribute to the appropriate person in a timely manner.
3. Do simple typing projects and make copies as directed by the administrative assistant.
4. Update the church master calendar. Coordinate calendar with administrative assistant.
5. Greet visitors.
6. File correspondence, reports, church newspaper ads, etc.
7. Duplicate and fold Sunday bulletins and monthly newsletters.
8. Open incoming mail and distribute to appropriate persons.
9. Apply postage; mail correspondence and newsletters.

CONGREGATIONAL CARE PASTOR

The congregational care pastor is responsible for building a sense of community in the church through reaching out to minister to the special needs of church members. This person will show the love of Christ in action.

Ministry Area/Department	General staff/administration
Position	Congregational care pastor
Accountable To	Pastor
Ministry Target	Church members
Position Is	Volunteer (with potential of becoming paid staff)
Position May Be Filled By	Church member
Minimum Maturity Level	Stable, maturing Christian
Spiritual Gifts	Pastor/shepherd • Mercy-showing • Exhortation
Talents or Abilities Desired	Good people skills
Best Personality Traits	Dependable • Good communicator • Discreet • Compassionate
Passion For	Uplifting and encouraging people • Creating a sense of community in the church
Length of Service Commitment	Two years minimum

ANTICIPATED TIME COMMITMENTS

1. **Doing ministry/preparing for ministry:** five hours a week
2. **Participating in meetings/training:** one hour a month

RESPONSIBILITIES/DUTIES

1. Follow up on sick, hospitalized or shut-in members; visit and contact regularly.
2. Pray for and with church members experiencing hardships or needing to make decisions.
3. Establish a support group for family members of the terminally ill.
4. Seek assistance for and offer support to the chronically ill.
5. Visit and offer emotional/spiritual support to grieving members.
6. Establish a chain of volunteers who will provide emotional, spiritual and physical help to the needy in the congregation: such as, prepare and deliver food on short-term basis, visit and pray with ill or grieving members, provide transportation, etc.
7. Inform pastor of special needs and report on those who are sick, hospitalized, experiencing financial difficulty, etc.
8. Remain in contact with prayer-group leaders regarding special prayer needs. (**Note:** Never share confidential information without the member's consent.)

9. Provide emotional and spiritual support to the unemployed. Seek help from church for financial needs, if necessary, with confidentiality.

10. Oversee committee and approve the disbursement of benevolence funds.

DEACON

A deacon is responsible for ministering to the needs of church members and offering support to the pastor.

Ministry Area/Department	General staff/administration
Position	Deacon
Accountable To	Pastor and/or congregational care pastor
Ministry Target	Church members
Position Is	Volunteer
Position May Be Filled By	Church member
Minimum Maturity Level	Stable, maturing Christian
Spiritual Gifts	Serving • Exhortation • Mercy-showing
Talents or Abilities Desired	Enjoy working with people
Best Personality Traits	Dependable • Compassionate • Discreet • Good moral character
Passion For	Ministering to the Body of Christ and assisting the pastor with the work of the ministry related to congregational care
Length of Service Commitment	Two years minimum

ANTICIPATED TIME COMMITMENTS

1. **Doing ministry/preparing for ministry:** four hours a week
2. **Participating in meetings/training:** five hours a month

RESPONSIBILITIES/DUTIES

1. Follow up on sick, hospitalized or shut-in members; visit and contact them regularly.
2. Pray for and with church members experiencing hardships or needing to make decisions.
3. Visit and offer emotional/spiritual support to grieving members.
4. Report special needs to the pastor, congregational care pastor, benevolence committee or other appropriate person.
5. Remain in contact with prayer-group leaders regarding special prayer needs. (**Note:** Never share confidential information without the person's consent.)
6. Rejoice with/congratulate members on special accomplishments and events.
7. Pray regularly for the leaders of the church.
8. Meet with and offer input to the pastor and appropriate staff members regarding any special or critical issues within the church.
9. Attend deacon meetings once or twice a month to discuss needs and budget items.

DRIVER OF CHURCH TRANSPORTATION

The driver of church transportation responsibilities will be distributed among several volunteers. A driver is responsible for safely transporting participants to and from church-related or church-sponsored activities.

Ministry Area/Department	General staff/administration
Position	Driver of church transportation
Accountable To	Executive pastor
Ministry Target	Church in general
Position Is	Volunteer
Position May Be Filled By	Church member
Minimum Maturity Level	New, growing Christian
Spiritual Gifts	Serving
Talents or Abilities Desired	Valid driver's license with good driving record • Able to drive church van—additional certification/special license required if driving a bus • Enjoy driving
Best Personality Traits	Dependable • Observant • Patient—no road-rage history! • Kindly
Passion For	Serving the church
Length of Service Commitment	One year minimum

ANTICIPATED TIME COMMITMENTS

1. **Doing ministry/preparing for ministry:** two hours a week
2. **Participating in meetings/training:** as needed

RESPONSIBILITIES/DUTIES

1. Shuttle seniors from nursing home to church and back on Sundays.
2. Provide transportation of various groups to special events, such as concerts, retreats, seminars, recreational activities, etc.
3. Pick up neighborhood children and adults without transportation for church activities (either Sunday morning, evening or during the week).
4. Pick up and return neighborhood children to and from Vacation Bible School—one week a year, during summer.

ELDER

The elders make up the church board—leading, shepherding and serving the church. Each elder heads a ministry committee in such areas as missions, youth, worship and senior ministry.

Ministry Area/Department	General staff/administration
Position	Elder
Accountable To	Pastor and church board
Ministry Target	Congregation
Position Is	Volunteer
Position May Be Filled By	Church member
Minimum Maturity Level	Stable, maturing Christian
Spiritual Gifts	Pastor/shepherd • Administration
Talents or Abilities Desired	Good organizational skills • Ability to lead others • Detail oriented • A spirit of discernment
Best Personality Traits	Leader-dependable or leader-analyst • Expresser
Passion For	Leading the church and serving its members
Length of Service Commitment	Three years minimum, depending on denomination

ANTICIPATED TIME COMMITMENTS

1. **Doing ministry/preparing for ministry:** four hours a week
2. **Participating in meetings/training:** five hours a month

RESPONSIBILITIES/DUTIES

1. Oversee activities of the church.
2. Along with the pastoral staff, provide leadership and vision for the church.
3. Work with ministry directors to head various ministries.
4. Meet twice a month, as part of the church board, to discuss and decide on church policy regarding whatever matters may arise between meetings.
5. Strive to follow the guidelines laid out in 1 Timothy 3 and Titus 1 concerning elders/overseers.
6. Pray regularly for the congregation.

EXECUTIVE ASSISTANT

The executive assistant is responsible for helping maintain an efficiently run office and assisting the executive pastor in the day-to-day office operations as well as with special projects.

Ministry Area/Department	General staff/administration
Position	Executive assistant
Accountable To	Executive pastor
Ministry Target	Church in general
Position Is	Paid staff
Position May Be Filled By	Church member
Minimum Maturity Level	New, growing Christian
Spiritual Gifts	Administration • Serving
Talents or Abilities Desired	Good organizational skills • Good people skills and phone manners • Computer keyboard and/or desktop publishing ability
Best Personality Traits	Dependable • Cheerful • Pleasant
Passion For	Efficiency and excellence in ministry and serving the church
Length of Service Commitment	Two years minimum

ANTICIPATED TIME COMMITMENTS

1. **Doing ministry/preparing for ministry:** forty hours a week
2. **Participating in meetings/training:** one hour a week

RESPONSIBILITIES/DUTIES

1. Perform receptionist duties: greet visitors, answer phone, screen and direct calls, take and deliver messages, get and route messages from answering machine/voice mail.
2. Open mail/handle correspondence for executive pastor.
3. Keep updated version of the church policies and procedures in print and on computer. Make changes and additions as directed.
4. Schedule appointments for pastoral staff.
5. Maintain prayer list of special requests from members and others.
6. Assist with planning and coordinating special events and banquets.
7. Assist with planning, developing and mailing newsletters, special brochures, etc.
8. Arrange for ad placements in local newspaper, etc.
9. Perform miscellaneous clerical duties as requested by the executive pastor.

EXECUTIVE PASTOR

The executive pastor is responsible for day-to-day church management and operations and will assist the senior pastor as needed with the ministry of the church.

Ministry Area/Department	General staff/administration
Position	Executive pastor
Accountable To	Pastor
Ministry Target	Church in general
Position Is	Paid staff
Position May Be Filled By	Church member (depending on the denomination)
Minimum Maturity Level	Solid, very mature Christian
Spiritual Gifts	Administration • Exhortation
Talents or Abilities Desired	Good organizational skills • Ability to teach or preach in pastor's absence • Ability to lead others
Best Personality Traits	Leader-dependable • Expresser
Passion For	Assisting the senior pastor in leading the church
Length of Service Commitment	Two years minimum

ANTICIPATED TIME COMMITMENTS

1. **Doing ministry/preparing for ministry:** forty hours a week, off on Saturday and one day during week, except for emergencies and special occasions
2. **Participating in meetings/training:** one hour minimum a week

RESPONSIBILITIES/DUTIES

1. Manage the church and church staff on a daily basis.
2. Conduct staff training and deal with personnel issues; report concerns to the senior pastor.
3. Ensure implementation of church policies and procedures.
4. Assist senior pastor in overseeing the ministries of the church; keep regular contact with ministry directors.
5. Preach in senior pastor's absence and on other occasions when asked by the pastor.
6. Pray for and support the senior pastor. Recommend solutions to ministry problems.
7. Participate in staff meetings and leadership training sessions.
8. Participate in visitation and outreach.
9. Help develop and oversee departmental budgets and monitor church budget.
10. Develop and recommend strategies for growth and program improvement.
11. Give final approval of church advertisements and printed materials.

FIRST-AID VOLUNTEER

The first-aid volunteer will be responsible to render first aid as needed during church services, activities and events. This person must show a caring and concerned spirit in calming and ministering to individuals who need first aid.

Ministry Area/Department	General staff/administration
Position	First-aid volunteer
Accountable To	Executive pastor or associate pastor
Ministry Target	Church in general
Position Is	Volunteer
Position May Be Filled By	Church member
Minimum Maturity Level	New, growing Christian
Spiritual Gifts	Mercy-showing • Serving
Talents or Abilities Desired	Certified nursing assistant, nurse, emergency medical technician, doctor or someone certified to give proper first-aid treatment • Current CPR certificate required.
Best Personality Traits	Compassionate • Careful • Levelheaded • Leader-analyst • Leader-dependable • Dependable-expresser
Passion For	Helping others
Length of Service Commitment	One year minimum

ANTICIPATED TIME COMMITMENTS
1. **Doing ministry/preparing for ministry**: as needed during church services/activities
2. **Participating in meetings/training**: as needed

RESPONSIBILITIES/DUTIES
1. Be available during church services, activities, events.
2. Provide first aid to members/visitors needing such services.
3. Transport or arrange transportation to the hospital when necessary.
4. Teach CPR (or arrange to have another qualified individual teach) to the pastoral staff, church leaders and congregation.

MISSIONS COORDINATOR

The missions coordinator will lead the effort to maintain a comprehensive missions program in the church and is responsible for exploring missions opportunities, keeping the church informed regarding potential and ongoing missions involvement and serving as a liaison between the church and missionaries.

Ministry Area/Department	Missions
Position	Missions coordinator
Accountable To	Pastor
Ministry Target	Local, national, world missionaries and non-Christians
Position Is	Volunteer
Position May Be Filled By	Church member
Minimum Maturity Level	Stable, maturing Christian
Spiritual Gifts	Administration • Pastor/shepherd • Evangelism • Giving • Mercy-showing
Talents or Abilities Desired	Good communication skills • Able to research, locate, validate and follow up on missions projects, opportunities and needs
Best Personality Traits	Committed • Compassionate • Analyst-dependable • Expresser
Passion For	Supporting and encouraging missionaries and evangelizing the lost throughout the world
Length of Service Commitment	Two years minimum

ANTICIPATED TIME COMMITMENTS

1. **Doing ministry/preparing for ministry**: two to four hours a month, more during special missions emphases
2. **Participating in meetings/training**: as needed

RESPONSIBILITIES/DUTIES

1. Act as a liaison with missionaries and organizations the church supports.
2. Research, locate, validate and follow up on missions projects, opportunities, needs within the local community as well as home and foreign mission fields.
3. Organize the church's efforts in supporting missions.
4. Educate the church regarding missions, including planning a yearly missions awareness emphasis.

RECORDS ADMINISTRATOR

The records administrator is responsible for keeping up-to-date records on church attendance and membership. These records will be available for examination by church leaders to help determine the state of the church and develop plans for spiritual and numerical growth as well as look at the need to expand the church's ministry or building facilities.

Ministry Area/Department	General staff/administration
Position	Records administrator
Accountable To	Pastor, executive pastor or assistant pastor
Ministry Target	Church in general
Position Is	Volunteer
Position May Be Filled By	Church member
Minimum Maturity Level	New, growing Christian
Spiritual Gifts	Administration
Talents or Abilities Desired	Accurate math skills • Attention to detail
Best Personality Traits	Dependable • Serious
Passion For	Facts and figures
Length of Service Commitment	One year minimum

ANTICIPATED TIME COMMITMENTS

1. Doing ministry/preparing for ministry: one to two hours a week
2. Participating in meetings/training: as needed

RESPONSIBILITIES/DUTIES

1. Compile all attendance records from various church department leaders, ushers, etc. and input totals/results in weekly, monthly and yearly reports.
2. Keep all reports, either in print or on computer disk, for future reference and comparison.
3. Keep an up-to-date record of all church members, adding statistics and information on new members as well as updating statistics and information when members transfer membership to another church.

SECURITY ASSISTANT

The security assistant is responsible for the overall security of the church facilities and people meeting in them.

Ministry Area/Department	General staff/administration
Position	Security assistant
Accountable To	Pastor, executive pastor or assistant pastor
Ministry Target	Church in general
Position Is	Volunteer
Position May Be Filled By	Other approved individual
Minimum Maturity Level	New, growing Christian
Spiritual Gifts	Exhortation • Serving
Talents or Abilities Desired	Alert • A spirit of discernment • Familiar with church facilities • Not easily intimidated
Best Personality Traits	Dependable • Serious • Levelheaded
Passion For	The welfare and safety of others
Length of Service Commitment	One year minimum

ANTICIPATED TIME COMMITMENTS

1. **Doing ministry/preparing for ministry:** one to two hours a week
2. **Participating in meetings/training:** as needed

RESPONSIBILITIES/DUTIES

1. Patrol church building and property during regular church services and major functions.
2. Report any incidents to proper authorities. Write a report of any related facts.
3. Greet strangers on the property and offer assistance: *May I help you find your way? Is there someone I could help you find? May I assist you with anything?*
4. Discreetly keep an eye on any suspicious situations or people.
5. Inform and seek assistance from other church leaders or from local authorities as needed in suspicious or potentially dangerous situations.

SENIOR PASTOR

The senior pastor shall serve as the chief undershepherd and overseer of this local church, feeding, leading and nurturing the sheep. This person's main responsibilities will be to communicate God's Word, minister to spiritual needs and provide biblical leadership for the church.

Ministry Area/Department	General staff/administration
Position	Senior pastor
Accountable To	God, church board (which may consist of deacons/elders, depending on the denomination)
Ministry Target	Church and community
Position Is	Paid staff
Position May Be Filled By	Church member (depending on the denomination)
Minimum Maturity Level	Stable, mature Christian
Spiritual Gifts	Pastor/shepherd • Exhortation • Teaching • Prophecy • Evangelism
Talents or Abilities Desired	Leadership ability • Good communicator • Experience in teaching and/or preaching • Some training or experience in counseling • Experience in leading others to Christ • Discreet
Best Personality Traits	Expresser • Caring
Passion For	Shepherding the saints, equipping them for ministry and influencing the community for Christ
Length of Service Commitment	Indefinite

ANTICIPATED TIME COMMITMENTS

1. **Doing ministry/preparing for ministry**: forty hours a week, off on Saturday and one day during week, except for emergencies and special occasions
2. **Participating in meetings/training**: one hour minimum a week

RESPONSIBILITIES/DUTIES

1. Oversee pastoral staff.
2. Provide leadership and vision for the church. Direct plans for ministry and church growth; develop and fine-tune the church structure based on the Team philosophy of ministry (see p. 20 for explanation of Team Ministry).
3. Motivate, equip and nurture the people of the church through example, preaching and teaching God's Word and spiritual counseling.
4. Spend significant time in prayer and Bible study.
5. Contact/visit hospitalized or grieving church members.

6. Officiate at weddings and funerals.

7. Provide premarital counseling, counseling regarding salvation and spiritual issues and other counseling for church members as time permits.

8. Perform sacraments such as Communion and baptism.

9. Oversee church discipline and manage conflict in the church. Seek to reconcile relationships and promote unity within the church.

10. Participate in evangelism efforts through preaching and giving invitations during worship services, revival or other special services, visitation and other outreach efforts.

Sunday School Director/Superintendent

The Sunday School director will lead and oversee the ministry of the Sunday School. This person will ensure proper staffing, training and operation of the department.

Ministry Area/Department	Sunday School
Position	Sunday School director/superintendent
Accountable To	Pastor
Ministry Target	Church
Position Is	Volunteer
Position May Be Filled By	Church member
Minimum Maturity Level	Stable, mature Christian
Spiritual Gifts	Administration • Exhortation
Talents or Abilities Desired	Good organizational and leadership skills
Best Personality Traits	Motivated • People oriented
Passion For	Reaching, teaching and nurturing people through Sunday School ministry
Length of Service Commitment	One year minimum

Anticipated Time Commitments

1. Doing ministry/preparing for ministry: three hours a week
2. Participating in meetings/training: one hour a month

Responsibilities/Duties

1. Recruit volunteers to serve in Sunday School ministry.
2. Develop and implement a training program for Sunday School leaders, teachers and workers.
3. Obtain information on Sunday School curricula; inform teachers of selection; order curricula.
4. Oversee distribution of Sunday School material or store it in a designated location for easy access by leaders.
5. Recognize, encourage and motivate Sunday School workers.
6. Communicate information regarding goals, special days, etc.
7. Oversee operation of Sunday School ministry (teachers on hand, lessons available, start/end on time, records procedures followed/forms completed, etc.).
8. Serve as a liaison between Sunday School and pastor.

TEAM MINISTRY COUNSELOR

The Team Ministry counselor will assist the Team Ministry director with interviewing members and recommending areas of service based on spiritual gifts, personalities and interests.

Ministry Area/Department	General/lay involvement
Position	Team Ministry counselor
Accountable To	Team Ministry director
Ministry Target	Church
Position Is	Volunteer
Position May Be Filled By	Church member
Minimum Maturity Level	Stable, mature Christian
Spiritual Gifts	Exhortation • Pastor/shepherd • Teaching
Talents or Abilities Desired	Able to communicate well with others
Best Personality Traits	Dependable • Expresser-analyst • Cooperative • Insightful
Passion For	Involving all Christians in the work of the ministry according to their individual spiritual gifts, personalities and interests
Length of Service Commitment	Two years minimum

ANTICIPATED TIME COMMITMENTS

1. **Doing ministry/preparing for ministry:** up to one hour a week
2. **Participating in meetings/training:** one hour each quarter or as needed

RESPONSIBILITIES/DUTIES

1. Become familiar with the Team philosophy of ministry and the Team Ministry course.
2. Become familiar with the ministry opportunities within and associated with this local church.
3. Interview people who complete the Team Ministry course to help them determine where they would best serve; make recommendations to the Team Ministry director.

TEAM MINISTRY DIRECTOR

The Team Ministry director will be responsible for placing people on the church team, based on their spiritual gifts, personalities and interests. This involves teaching the Team Ministry course[1] and administering spiritual gifts inventories in order to help members identify and understand their gifts and how they can be used in ministry and advising members of ministry opportunities within the church and related ministries.

Ministry Area/Department	General/lay involvement
Position	Team Ministry director
Accountable To	Pastor or executive pastor
Ministry Target	Church
Position Is	Volunteer
Position May Be Filled By	Church member
Minimum Maturity Level	Stable, mature Christian
Spiritual Gifts	Exhortation • Pastor/shepherd • Administration • Teaching
Talents or Abilities Desired	Able to coordinate and harmonize a group of people
Best Personality Traits	Dependable • Cooperative • Expresser-leader
Passion For	Involving all Christians in the work of the ministry according to their individual spiritual gifts, personalities and interests
Length of Service Commitment	Two years minimum

ANTICIPATED TIME COMMITMENTS

1. **Doing ministry/preparing for ministry**: two hours a week
2. **Participating in meetings/training**: one hour each quarter or as needed

RESPONSIBILITIES/DUTIES

1. Become familiar with the Team philosophy of ministry and the Team Ministry course.
2. Become familiar with the ministry opportunities within and associated with this local church and maintain an updated list of available positions and tasks.
3. Teach the Team Ministry course at least twice a year for newcomers, new Christians, and current members who want a refresher—or train someone else to teach the course).
4. Administer the spiritual gifts inventory to all church members, especially new members.
5. Interview people who complete the Team Ministry course to help them find their place on the team based on their spiritual gifts, personalities and interests. Team Ministry counselors may be recruited to assist with this interviewing process.
6. Keep a record of who is serving in each position.

ADULT BIBLE STUDY TEACHER

The adult Bible study teacher is the shepherd of the class and is responsible for keeping watch over the flock and overseeing or coordinating all class leaders and functions. The teacher is expected to teach, reach and minister to members and prospects with the help of other leaders within the class.

Ministry Area/Department	Adult Sunday School
Position	Adult Bible study teacher
Accountable To	Sunday School director
Ministry Target	Adults
Position Is	Volunteer
Position May Be Filled By	Church member
Minimum Maturity Level	Stable, maturing Christian
Spiritual Gifts	Shepherding • Teaching • Exhortation
Talents or Abilities Desired	Ability to communicate well with others • Able to speak in front of a group.
Best Personality Traits	Dependable-leader • Expresser • Compassionate
Passion For	Teaching and leading a group of people • Discipling others
Length of Service Commitment	One year minimum

ANTICIPATED TIME COMMITMENTS

1. Doing ministry/preparing for ministry: three hours a week
2. Participating in meetings/training: one hour a month

RESPONSIBILITIES/DUTIES

1. Participate in teachers' meetings and training opportunities.
2. Work with Sunday School director to choose curriculum for your class.
3. Study and prepare for each weekly lesson.
4. Pray for class members/visitors.
5. Arrive 15 minutes before class begins to make sure classroom is prepared and to greet people as they arrive.
6. Lead each week's class and involve participants in studying and learning God's Word through various teaching methods.
7. Promote spiritual growth and unity among class members.
8. Organize class into care groups of six people or less with one leader per group.

ADULT CLASS CARE GROUP LEADER

The adult class care group leader is responsible for encouraging care group members, discovering spiritual and physical needs of care group members and seeing that needs are met. This person promotes unity, support and accountability within the group.

Ministry Area/Department	Adult Sunday School
Position	Adult class care group leader
Accountable To	Adult Bible study teacher
Ministry Target	Adults
Position Is	Volunteer
Position May Be Filled By	Church member
Minimum Maturity Level	Stable, mature Christian
Spiritual Gifts	Exhortation • Serving • Mercy-showing
Talents or Abilities Desired	A people person • Able to communicate well, good listener • Discreet • Gets along well with others.
Best Personality Traits	Compassionate • Sociable • Dependable-expresser or expresser-analyst
Passion For	The spiritual and physical well-being of fellow class members
Length of Service Commitment	One year minimum

ANTICIPATED TIME COMMITMENTS

1. **Doing ministry/preparing for ministry**: one hour a week
2. **Participating in meetings/training**: yearly training/inspirational workshop

RESPONSIBILITIES/DUTIES

1. Participate in training opportunities.
2. Look for/be informed of ministry needs within your care group.
3. Contact members of your care group on a regular basis to encourage them. Note any needs expressed or observed. Involve appropriate staff in meeting needs.
4. Contact absent care-group members to make sure everything is all right.
5. Perform ministry actions for care-group members and involve other members in ministry to one another.
6. Initiate follow-up contacts regarding special needs when appropriate.
7. Pray regularly for your care-group members.
8. Participate in a class prayer chain. When called by the teacher, prayer leader or other member, contact your care-group members to inform them of special prayer need. You

may want to call one care-group member, then have that member call another member and so on.

9. Witness to unsaved class members and lead unchurched Christian members to unite with the church. Involve outreach leader when needed.

ADULT CLASS FELLOWSHIP LEADER

The adult class fellowship leader is responsible for planning and coordinating all class social events at church or elsewhere and for recruiting class members to help as needed. This leader will promote unity among the group.

Ministry Area/Department	Adult Sunday School
Position	Adult class fellowship leader
Accountable To	Adult Bible study teacher
Ministry Target	Adults
Position Is	Volunteer
Position May Be Filled By	Church member
Minimum Maturity Level	New, growing Christian
Spiritual Gifts	Administration • Serving • Exhortation
Talents or Abilities Desired	Ability to organize events and motivate people
Best Personality Traits	Outgoing • Sociable • Expresser-dependable
Passion For	Promoting unity and planning special events
Length of Service Commitment	One year minimum

ANTICIPATED TIME COMMITMENTS:

1. **Doing ministry/preparing for ministry:** one hour a month
2. **Participating in meetings/training:** yearly training/inspirational workshop

RESPONSIBILITIES/DUTIES

1. Participate in training opportunities.
2. Plan, coordinate and lead class social events.
3. Encourage get-acquainted or icebreaker activities within the class.
4. Plan for serving occasional—or even weekly—refreshments before class.

ADULT CLASS PRAYER LEADER

The adult class prayer leader is responsible for praying fervently, organizing and leading a class prayer chain and encouraging spiritual growth in class members through daily devotions and prayer.

Ministry Area/Department	Adult Sunday School
Position	Adult class prayer leader
Accountable To	Adult Bible study teacher
Ministry Target	Adults
Position Is	Volunteer
Position May Be Filled By	Church member
Minimum Maturity Level	Stable, maturing Christian
Spiritual Gifts	Exhortation • Mercy-showing • Pastor/shepherd
Talents or Abilities Desired	Ability to communicate well with others • Organized
Best Personality Traits	Caring • Serious • Discreet • Dependable-leader
Passion For	Praying • The importance and power of prayer
Length of Service Commitment	One year minimum

ANTICIPATED TIME COMMITMENTS

1. **Doing ministry/preparing for ministry:** three hours a week
2. **Participating in meetings/training:** one hour a week (prayer meeting)

RESPONSIBILITIES/DUTIES

1. Pray daily for the needs of members and prospects. Also, pray for church-related activities and ministries and for church leaders.
2. Organize a class prayer chain through the care-group leaders to inform class members of special or urgent prayer needs.
3. Encourage class members to pray for foreign and home missions.
4. Provide or recommend devotional material and exhort members to have daily devotions, personally and with their families.

ADULT CLASS SECRETARY

The adult class secretary is responsible for keeping accurate, up-to-date records; seeing that appropriate forms are completed regarding enrollment changes, visitors, etc.; preparing or assisting with class correspondence when needed and welcoming newcomers to the class.

Ministry Area/Department	Adult Sunday School
Position	Adult class secretary
Accountable To	Adult Bible study teacher
Ministry Target	Adults
Position Is	Volunteer
Position May Be Filled By	Church member
Minimum Maturity Level	New, growing Christian
Spiritual Gifts	Administration • Serving
Talents or Abilities Desired	Organized • Attention to detail • Good penmanship
Best Personality Traits	Dependable
Passion For	Organization, accuracy and serving as a support person
Length of Service Commitment	One year minimum

ANTICIPATED TIME COMMITMENTS

1. **Doing ministry/preparing for ministry**: one hour a week
2. **Participating in meetings/training**: yearly training workshop

RESPONSIBILITIES/DUTIES

1. Participate in training opportunities, yearly or when presented.
2. Keep accurate records of member attendance and up-to-date personal information (address, phone, birthday, etc.).
3. Welcome visitors and help new members feel accepted.
4. Ask visitors to complete appropriate forms or personally register them in your class by obtaining their names, addresses and phone numbers and determining whether or not they are members of another church.
5. Keep records of visitor and prospect information for outreach purposes. Have this information readily available to the teacher, outreach leader and other concerned staff.
6. Complete weekly attendance form, collect class offerings and turn them in to adult records clerk.
7. Prepare or assist with special correspondence to class members.

ADULT RECORDS CLERK

The adult records clerk is responsible for accurately calculating weekly attendance and offering totals for the adult department and for delivering offerings and visitor information to the appropriate staff members.

Ministry Area/Department	Adult Sunday School
Position	Adult records clerk
Accountable To	Adult Bible study teacher
Ministry Target	Adults
Position Is	Volunteer
Position May Be Filled By	Church member
Minimum Maturity Level	Stable, maturing Christian
Spiritual Gifts	Administration • Serving
Talents or Abilities Desired	Organized • Detail oriented • Good math skills
Best Personality Traits	Dependable
Passion For	Organization, accuracy and good stewardship
Length of Service Commitment	One year minimum

ANTICIPATED TIME COMMITMENTS

1. **Doing ministry/preparing for ministry**: one hour a week
2. **Participating in meetings/training**: yearly training workshop

RESPONSIBILITIES/DUTIES

1. Participate in training opportunities yearly, or as presented.
2. Tally class attendance records to obtain weekly attendance figures.
3. Calculate and record total of all classes' tithes and offerings.
4. Deliver all tithes and offerings to treasurer, bookkeeper or appropriate person as set forth in church policy.
5. Assemble visitor forms received from classes and deliver them to the church outreach director or other designated person.

BUILDINGS AND GROUNDS

BUILDINGS AND GROUNDS ADMINISTRATOR

The buildings and grounds administrator is responsible for the general upkeep and oversight of the church property and supervision of the church custodian. This person may arrange for yearly church clean-up days in which church volunteers assist with special projects. In the event of weddings, funerals and other nonchurch-sponsored events, the event host will be responsible for paying for the administrator's services as needed. Church policy will dictate fees.

Ministry Area/Department	Buildings and grounds
Position	Buildings and grounds administrator
Accountable To	Executive pastor
Ministry Target	Church in general
Position Is	Paid staff
Position May Be Filled By	Other approved individual
Minimum Maturity Level	Stable, maturing Christian
Spiritual Gifts	Serving • Administration
Talents or Abilities Desired	General construction • Building maintenance • Lawn-care skills • Ability to supervise others • Valid driver's license and transportation
Best Personality Traits	Dependable • Hardworking • Initiative to get things done without direct supervision • Analyst-dependable or analyst-expresser
Passion For	Good stewardship of the facilities God has given the church • Presenting a positive physical appearance of the church in the community
Length of Service Commitment	Two years minimum

ANTICIPATED TIME COMMITMENTS

1. **Doing ministry/preparing for ministry:** forty to forty-five hours a week
2. **Participating in meetings/training:** two hours a month

RESPONSIBILITIES/DUTIES

1. General oversight of buildings and grounds maintenance; ensuring safe, clean and proper order of the facilities. Keep a record of regular maintenance done on buildings/grounds and a list of projects to do.
2. Order and maintain supplies for cleaning, maintaining and repairing building/grounds.
3. Make building repairs such as plumbing, electrical, carpentry, painting, and arrange for outside repair services when necessary.
4. Maintain lawn and arrange snow/ice/debris removal from parking areas, sidewalks, steps, etc.

5. Fill/drain baptistry as needed.
6. Operate heating and cooling equipment (ensure proper settings for any events held in the facilities and adjust settings for times the facilities may not be in use).
7. Set up and take down chairs/partitions as needed for weekly services, meetings and special functions.
8. Oversee custodian. Ensure that building is kept clean.
9. Manage all keys to the facilities. Keep a master of each key. Obtain new keys when needed.
10. Ensure church security; lock and unlock facilities for church services and events.
11. Ensure that church vehicles are maintained.
12. Oversee budget and expenditures for buildings and grounds.

BUILDINGS CUSTODIAN

The buildings custodian is responsible for keeping the church buildings clean and orderly. In the event of weddings, funerals and other nonchurch sponsored events, the event host will be responsible for paying for the custodian's services. Church policy will dictate fees.

Ministry Area/Department	Buildings and grounds
Position	Buildings custodian
Accountable To	Buildings and grounds administrator
Ministry Target	Church in general
Position Is	Paid staff
Position May Be Filled By	Other approved individual
Minimum Maturity Level	New, growing Christian
Spiritual Gifts	Serving
Talents or Abilities Desired	Able to perform physical labor necessary in cleaning church facilities
Best Personality Traits	Hardworking • Conscientious • Analyst-dependable or leader-dependable
Passion For	Good stewardship of the facilities God has given the church • Present a positive physical appearance of the church in the community
Length of Service Commitment	One year minimum

ANTICIPATED TIME COMMITMENTS

1. **Doing ministry/preparing for ministry:** twenty to forty hours a week
2. **Participating in meetings/training:** one hour a month

RESPONSIBILITIES/DUTIES

1. Inform buildings and grounds administrator when cleaning supplies are low or when equipment or facilities need repair.
2. Empty all wastebaskets weekly; more often if necessary.
3. Dust furniture in offices, reception areas, visitor center, sanctuary and entrances.
4. Vacuum offices and carpeted areas weekly, or more often if needed. Dust-mop, sweep or vacuum other areas as needed.
5. Clean/disinfect drinking fountains and telephone mouthpieces weekly.
6. Clean cobwebs from ceilings, corners, vents, fans, etc. as needed.
7. Thoroughly clean restrooms weekly. Check them after each event and reclean if necessary—includes cleaning toilet bowls, urinals, partitions, tiled walls, mirrors and floors and

refilling soap, towel and toilet paper dispensers, making sure toilet paper and paper towels are available and emptying trash and sanitary containers.

8. Clean windows and glass doors as needed.

9. Replace light bulbs. Turn off nonrequired lights.

10. Water plants as needed.

11. Pick up litter.

12. Check all areas for odors. Clean/disinfect as necessary.

13. Clean up after church-sponsored special events.

14. Clean up accidents as needed: spills, stomach upset, etc.

15. Check and clean baptistry area after baptisms and as needed.

16. Straighten hymnals and restock pew racks on Mondays and after midweek meetings and services.

GARDENING ASSISTANT

The gardening assistant will contribute to the beauty and physical appearance of the church by planting and helping maintain flower gardens on the property.

Ministry Area/Department	Buildings and grounds
Position	Gardening assistant
Accountable To	Groundskeeper/buildings and grounds administrator
Ministry Target	Church in general
Position Is	Volunteer
Position May Be Filled By	Regular attendee
Minimum Maturity Level	New, growing Christian
Spiritual Gifts	Serving
Talents or Abilities Desired	Landscaping and gardening experience a plus but not required • Able to do light physical work and enjoy gardening
Best Personality Traits	Outdoor person • Initiative to finish tasks • Leader-dependable
Passion For	Beautiful flower gardens
Length of Service Commitment	One year minimum

ANTICIPATED TIME COMMITMENTS

1. **Doing ministry/preparing for ministry:** one to two hours a week, depending on season/weather—a full day in spring for planting
2. **Participating in meetings/training:** as needed

RESPONSIBILITIES/DUTIES

1. Help prepare garden spots; add new soil, fertilizer and work ground as needed.
2. Plant shrubs/flowers/trees.
3. Weed flower gardens, or assist groundskeeper in this task.
4. Prune rosebushes, dust for diseases and insects as necessary or assist groundskeeper.
5. Routinely check on gardens to insure proper upkeep and beauty.

GROUNDSKEEPER

The groundskeeper will work to improve and maintain a well-kept, neat appearance of the church grounds.

Ministry Area/Department	Buildings and grounds
Position	Groundskeeper
Accountable To	Buildings and grounds administrator
Ministry Target	Church in general
Position Is	Paid staff
Position May Be Filled By	Other approved individual
Minimum Maturity Level	New, growing Christian
Spiritual Gifts	Serving
Talents or Abilities Desired	Landscaping experience a plus, but not required • Ability to use lawn equipment • Enjoy working with hands, working outside, lawn and garden tasks • Able to do physical labor
Best Personality Traits	Dependable-expresser or leader-dependable • Hardworking
Passion For	Maintaining a beautiful lawn, thereby giving a positive impression of the church and glorifying God through emphasizing the beauty of His creation
Length of Service Commitment	One year minimum

ANTICIPATED TIME COMMITMENTS

1. **Doing ministry/preparing for ministry**: eight hours minimum a week
2. **Participating in meetings/training**: as needed

RESPONSIBILITIES/DUTIES

1. Cut the grass weekly or as needed, depending on the seasons.
2. Trim around shrubs, foundations—anywhere needed.
3. Spread fertilizer and weed and crabgrass preventer twice a year or as necessary.
4. Trim shrubs.
5. Weed and water flower gardens.
6. Clear snow/ice/debris from walkways; put down ice-melting crystals to prevent slick spots when necessary.
7. Pick up litter from grounds.
8. Maintain lawn and garden equipment; arrange for repairs when needed.
9. Order/pick up lawn and garden supplies when needed.

CHILDREN

BIG BUDDY

The Big Buddy is responsible for making a positive difference in a child's life through offering encouragement and planning special activities with the parent's or guardian's approval.

Ministry Area/Department	Children
Position	Big Buddy
Accountable To	Children's pastor or Big Buddy coordinator
Ministry Target	Children
Position Is	Volunteer
Position May Be Filled By	Church member
Minimum Maturity Level	New, growing Christian
Spiritual Gifts	Pastor/shepherd • Teaching
Talents or Abilities Desired	Enjoy activities with children • Must be a good role model with no criminal record
Best Personality Traits	Dependable-expresser
Passion For	Encouraging children and having a positive influence on their lives
Length of Service Commitment	One year minimum

ANTICIPATED TIME COMMITMENTS

1. **Doing ministry/preparing for ministry**: fifteen minutes to six hours a week
2. **Participating in meetings/training**: yearly training workshop

RESPONSIBILITIES/DUTIES

1. Participate in training opportunities yearly, or as presented.
2. Serve as a Big Buddy to a child of a single-parent home. When Mom is gone, mother figure is needed. When Dad is gone, father figure is needed.
3. Contact the child by phone at least once a week to touch base, offer encouragement and ask how things are going.
4. Talk with the child's parent or guardian to get approval for plans to take the child somewhere special or to participate in fun activities.
5. Plan activities with the child at least once a month. Activities should be something the child enjoys and may include, but are not limited to
   a. Going to sporting events
   b. Going fishing
   c. Going out for ice cream or lunch and to the park, playground or a movie
   d. Making crafts
   e. Going bowling

    f. Help with a special school project

6. Recognize the child's birthday and special accomplishments. Offer praise, send a card, give a gift, attend an event or in some way show you care.

7. Pray regularly for the child.

BIG BUDDY COORDINATOR

The Big Buddy coordinator is responsible for developing and overseeing the Big Buddy program and ensuring proper training and safety for both the child and the Big Buddy.

Ministry Area/Department	Children
Position	Big Buddy coordinator
Accountable To	Children's pastor
Ministry Target	Children
Position Is	Volunteer
Position May Be Filled By	Church member
Minimum Maturity Level	Stable, maturing Christian
Spiritual Gifts	Administration • Mercy-showing • Pastor/shepherd
Talents or Abilities Desired	Have a heart for children of single-parent homes • Must be a good role model with no criminal record • Good organizational skills
Best Personality Traits	Dependable-expresser
Passion For	Providing a safe environment and a positive influence in children's lives
Length of Service Commitment	One year minimum

ANTICIPATED TIME COMMITMENTS
1. **Doing ministry/preparing for ministry:** one hour a week
2. **Participating in meetings/training:** yearly training workshop

RESPONSIBILITIES/DUTIES
1. Participate in training opportunities yearly, or as presented.
2. Recruit and provide training to Big Buddies.
3. Run a criminal background check on people who volunteer to serve as Big Buddies, and check references before approving individuals as Big Buddies. Volunteers must sign a release for you to do the background check.
4. Conduct orientation and training session for all new Big Buddy volunteers who are approved.
5. Talk with children's pastor and social services to locate children in need who would fit the program.
6. Match children with Big Buddies.
7. Coordinate and oversee the Big Buddy program.
8. Pray for the children and the Big Buddies.

CHILDREN'S CHURCH ASSISTANT

The children's church assistant is a right arm to the children's church leader. As such, he or she will help keep order among the children in children's church and will assist with miscellaneous duties as needed.

Ministry Area/Department	Children's church
Position	Children's church assistant
Accountable To	Children's church leader
Ministry Target	Children (ages 5 to 11)
Position Is	Volunteer
Position May Be Filled By	Church member
Minimum Maturity Level	New, growing Christian
Spiritual Gifts	Serving • Exhortation
Talents or Abilities Desired	Able to communicate well with children
Best Personality Traits	Dependable • Compassionate
Passion For	Influencing children's lives with God's love and message
Length of Service Commitment	One year minimum

ANTICIPATED TIME COMMITMENTS

1. **Doing ministry/preparing for ministry**: one-and-a-half hours a week
2. **Participating in meetings/training**: one hour a month or as requested

RESPONSIBILITIES/DUTIES

1. Participate in training opportunities yearly, or as presented.
2. When requested, assist children's church leader in preparing for the weekly program.
3. Assist children's church leader, as needed, with weekly children's church program. This may include directing portions of the program or working up front with the leader, performing miscellaneous duties.
4. Help keep order in the service; set an example for the children by following the directions and requests the leader makes of the children.
5. Pray for the children.

CHILDREN'S CHURCH CHAPERONE

The children's church chaperone is responsible for overseeing the children to insure a safe and orderly children's church program.

Ministry Area/Department	Children's church
Position	Children's church chaperone
Accountable To	Children's church leader
Ministry Target	Children (ages 5 to 11)
Position Is	Volunteer
Position May Be Filled By	Church member
Minimum Maturity Level	New, growing Christian
Spiritual Gifts	Serving • Exhortation
Talents or Abilities Desired	Able to communicate well with children
Best Personality Traits	Patient • Consistent • Dependable
Passion For	Influencing children's lives with God's love and message
Length of Service Commitment	One year minimum

ANTICIPATED TIME COMMITMENTS

1. **Doing ministry/preparing for ministry:** one-and-a-half hours a week
2. **Participating in meetings/training:** yearly workshop or upon request

RESPONSIBILITIES/DUTIES

1. Participate in training opportunities yearly, or as presented.
2. Help keep order in the service:
   a. Keep children away from equipment.
   b. Greet children; direct them to the restroom or water fountain when necessary, preferably before program begins.
   c. Direct younger children to the front and older children to the back of the room or auditorium.
   d. Oversee children during the program. Encourage participation and discreetly administer discipline when necessary. Refer to the children's ministry policy on discipline. We do not use physical punishment as a form of discipline in the church.
   e. Dismiss children by rows or groups. Help them gather their belongings. Younger children should remain in a designated area, under supervision, until a parent or responsible adult arrives for them.
3. Distribute handouts and prizes when they are used.
4. Pray for the children.

CHILDREN'S CHURCH LEADER

The children's church leader is responsible for planning and leading exciting weekly children's church services.

Ministry Area/Department	Children's church
Position	Children's church leader
Accountable To	Children's ministry director
Ministry Target	Children (ages 5 to 11)
Position Is	Volunteer
Position May Be Filled By	Church member
Minimum Maturity Level	Stable, mature Christian
Spiritual Gifts	Exhortation • Pastor/Shepherd
Talents or Abilities Desired	Enthusiastic speaker • Musical abilities a plus
Best Personality Traits	Cheerful • Energetic • Compassionate • Expresser-leader
Passion For	Influencing children's lives with God's love and message
Length of Service Commitment	One year minimum

ANTICIPATED TIME COMMITMENTS

1. **Doing ministry/preparing for ministry**: two-and-a-half hours a week
2. **Participating in meetings/training**: one hour a month

RESPONSIBILITIES/DUTIES

1. Participate in training opportunities yearly, or as presented.
2. Work with appropriate church staff or volunteers to construct or obtain props or materials needed for the children's church program.
3. Plan and lead weekly children's church program.
4. Coordinate with special speakers, puppeteers, musicians and any other ministers who will take part in the children's church program.
5. Pray for children and workers. Lead prayer in children's church.
6. Lead songs during children's church or recruit a song leader/music director for children's church. Develop a rotating song list and frequently learn and teach new songs to the children.
7. Work with children's ministry director to select or develop the curriculum for children's church.

CHILDREN'S CLASS SECRETARY

The children's class secretary is responsible for keeping accurate, up-to-date records; seeing that appropriate forms are completed regarding enrollment changes, visitors, etc.; preparing or assisting with class correspondence when needed; and welcoming students to the class.

Ministry Area/Department	Children's Sunday School
Position	Children's class secretary
Accountable To	Children's teacher
Ministry Target	Children (ages 5 to 11)
Position Is	Volunteer
Position May Be Filled By	Church member
Minimum Maturity Level	New, growing Christian
Spiritual Gifts	Administration • Serving
Talents or Abilities Desired	Good organizational skills • Detail oriented • Good penmanship
Best Personality Traits	Dependable-analyst • Cheerful
Passion For	Encouraging children and serving as a support person to ensure organization and accuracy
Length of Service Commitment	One year minimum

ANTICIPATED TIME COMMITMENTS

1. **Doing ministry/preparing for ministry:** one hour a week
2. **Participating in meetings/training:** yearly training workshop

RESPONSIBILITIES/DUTIES

1. Participate in training opportunities yearly, or as presented.
2. Keep accurate attendance records and up-to-date personal information (address, phone, birthday, etc.).
3. Welcome visitors, help new members feel accepted and greet all attendees.
4. Prepare name tags for class leaders and for visitors as they arrive.
5. Register visitors in your class, obtaining name, address, phone number and determining whether or not their families are members of other churches.
6. Keep record of visitor and prospect information for outreach purposes. Have this information readily available to the teacher, outreach leader or other concerned staff.
7. Complete weekly attendance form, collect class offerings and turn them in to children's ministry records clerk.
8. Prepare or assist with correspondence to class members.

CHILDREN'S MINISTRY ACTIVITIES DIRECTOR

The children's ministry activities director is responsible to plan and carry out special events and activities outside the normal children's church and Sunday School program. These activities should motivate and excite children, keeping them interested in the church and Christian life while offering them a safe environment for having fun.

Ministry Area/Department	Children's ministry
Position	Children's ministry activities director
Accountable To	Children's ministry director
Ministry Target	Children (ages 5 to 11)
Position Is	Volunteer
Position May Be Filled By	Church member
Minimum Maturity Level	New, growing Christian
Spiritual Gifts	Administration • Exhortation
Talents or Abilities Desired	Good organizational skills • Familiar with what appeals to children
Best Personality Traits	Analyst-dependable or expresser-leader • Outgoing
Passion For	Children's safety and happiness
Length of Service Commitment	One year minimum

ANTICIPATED TIME COMMITMENTS

1. **Doing ministry/preparing for ministry:** four to eight hours a month
2. **Participating in meetings/training:** one hour a month

RESPONSIBILITIES/DUTIES

1. Participate in training opportunities as offered.
2. Research or create special events and activities that children would enjoy.
3. Plan special seasonal and monthly activities for children.
   a. Fellowship and fun activities at church and away from church
   b. Evangelistic activities, inviting unchurched friends to participate
4. Develop list of supplies needed and seek approval and funds from the children's ministry director.
5. Enlist help to carry out events and activities.
6. Pray for the children.

CHILDREN'S MINISTRY DIRECTOR

The children's ministry director is responsible to oversee the entire children's ministry to ensure a smoothly operating, safe and effective program. The director will recruit and train leaders who will touch children's lives with God's love, teach them God's Word and provide fellowship with God's people—laying a foundation that will keep children interested in the things of God and involved in church.

Ministry Area/Department	Children's ministry
Position	Children's ministry director
Accountable To	Pastor
Ministry Target	Children (ages 5 to 11)
Position Is	Volunteer (or paid, depending on church size, budget and workload of position)
Position May Be Filled By	Church member
Minimum Maturity Level	Stable, maturing Christian
Spiritual Gifts	Administration • Evangelism • Pastor/shepherd
Talents or Abilities Desired	Good organizational skills • Ability to motivate people • Good communicator.
Best Personality Traits	Dependable • Expresser-leader
Passion For	Influencing and affecting children's lives with the gospel of Christ
Length of Service Commitment	Two years minimum

ANTICIPATED TIME COMMITMENTS

1. **Doing ministry/preparing for ministry**: four hours a week or more, depending on church size/scope of ministry
2. **Participating in meetings/training**: one hour a week

RESPONSIBILITIES/DUTIES

1. Participate in training opportunities as offered.
2. Oversee and coordinate all aspects of the children's ministry.
3. Organize training and planning sessions for children's leaders/workers.
4. Screen children's workers and leaders before placing them in ministry.
   a. Have everyone complete an application and sign a release form for a police background check. This is a safety precaution for the children's sake. Plus, many insurance companies now require such procedures in order to insure the church against liability relating to misconduct.
   b. Proceed with background check and file results in a confidential folder to be kept in a locked file cabinet in the church office.

   c. Approve or disapprove workers and leaders for service in the children's ministry.

5. Investigate any complaints regarding children's ministry workers. Discuss complaints/problems with workers when warranted. Document and report serious matters to pastor and proper authorities.

6. Approve all children's ministries programs, curricula, activities and disbursement of funds for supplies and projects, keeping within budgeted amount.

7. Work with children's church leader to plan weekly programs and participate as needed. Lead devotional time or special part in weekly service, either on a regular basis or as an occasional special guest.

8. Be available to counsel and pray with children regarding spiritual matters.

9. Pray for the children and children's ministry workers.

CHILDREN'S MINISTRY RECORDS CLERK

The children's ministry records clerk is responsible for accurately calculating weekly attendance and offering totals for the children's department and for delivering offerings and visitor information to the appropriate staff members.

Ministry Area/Department	Children's ministry
Position	Children's ministry records clerk
Accountable To	Children's ministry director
Ministry Target	Children (ages 5 to 11)
Position Is	Volunteer
Position May Be Filled By	Church member
Minimum Maturity Level	New, growing Christian
Spiritual Gifts	Administration • Serving
Talents or Abilities Desired	Good organizational and math skills • Detail oriented
Best Personality Traits	Dependable-analyst
Passion For	Organization, accuracy and good stewardship
Length of Service Commitment	One year minimum

ANTICIPATED TIME COMMITMENTS

1. **Doing ministry/preparing for ministry:** one hour a week
2. **Participating in meetings/training:** yearly training workshop

RESPONSIBILITIES/DUTIES

1. Participate in training opportunities, yearly or as presented.
2. Tally class attendance records to obtain weekly attendance figures.
3. Calculate total of all classes' tithes and offerings and record information.
4. Deliver all tithes and offerings to treasurer or appropriate person as set forth in church policy.
5. Assemble visitor forms received from classes and deliver them to the church outreach director or other designated person.

CHILDREN'S TEACHER

The children's teacher is the shepherd of the class and is responsible to keep watch over the flock and oversee or coordinate all class leaders and functions. The teacher is expected to teach, reach and minister to members and prospects, with the help of other leaders within the class.

Ministry Area/Department	Children's Sunday School
Position	Children's teacher
Accountable To	Children's ministry director or Sunday School director, depending on church structure
Ministry Target	Children (ages 5 to 11)
Position Is	Volunteer
Position May Be Filled By	Church member
Minimum Maturity Level	Stable, maturing Christian
Spiritual Gifts	Shepherding • Teaching • Exhortation
Talents or Abilities Desired	Ability to communicate well with children
Best Personality Traits	Expresser-leader • Dependable • Compassionate
Passion For	Nurturing a group of children • Teaching and leading them to Jesus
Length of Service Commitment	One year minimum

ANTICIPATED TIME COMMITMENTS

1. **Doing ministry/preparing for ministry**: three hours a week
2. **Participating in meetings/training**: one hour a month

RESPONSIBILITIES/DUTIES

1. Participate in teacher's meetings and training opportunities.
2. Work with the director to choose curriculum for your class.
3. Study and prepare for each weekly lesson. Gather necessary materials: handouts, craft supplies, etc.
4. Pray for class members/visitors.
5. Arrive 15 minutes before class begins to make sure classroom is prepared and to greet children as they arrive.
6. Lead each week's class time and involve children in studying and learning God's Word through various teaching methods and activities.
7. Promote spiritual growth and unity among class members.
8. Maintain contact with children and parents. Keep parents informed of topics/themes being studied, special events, etc. through printed notices, postcards and calls. Call, visit or send cards to students on special occasions or when a student is sick; class secretary can assist with these duties also.

CHILDREN'S TEACHER ASSISTANT

The children's teacher assistant is the right arm of the children's teacher. The assistant must be prepared to fill in for the teacher when necessary and assist with keeping watch over the flock and coordinating class functions. The assistant is expected to teach, reach and minister to members and prospects, under the direction of the teacher.

Ministry Area/Department	Children's Sunday School
Position	Children's teacher assistant
Accountable To	Children's teacher
Ministry Target	Children (ages 5 to 11)
Position Is	Volunteer
Position May Be Filled By	Church member
Minimum Maturity Level	New, growing Christian
Spiritual Gifts	Shepherding • Serving • Exhortation
Talents or Abilities Desired	Ability to communicate well with children • Able to allow someone else to lead, but willing to take the lead when necessary
Best Personality Traits	Dependable-leader or dependable-expresser
Passion For	Discipling children and providing support for other leaders
Length of Service Commitment	One year minimum

ANTICIPATED TIME COMMITMENTS

1. **Doing ministry/preparing for ministry:** two hours a week
2. **Participating in meetings/training:** one hour a month

RESPONSIBILITIES/DUTIES

1. Participate in teacher's meetings and training opportunities.
2. Study each weekly lesson and be available to lead the class in the teacher's absence.
3. Assist teacher with preparing materials for class: handouts, craft supplies, etc.
4. Distribute handouts to children; help children with crafts or activities as needed.
5. Escort children to the restroom if it is not connected to the classroom. Assist younger children as needed; insure hand washing. **Note:** It might be best if a woman is responsible for this task.
6. Pray for class members and visitors.
7. Promote spiritual growth and unity among class members.

MISSIONS STUDY DIRECTOR

The missions study director is responsible for planning and overseeing the children's missions study program.

Ministry Area/Department	Children's ministry
Position	Missions study director
Accountable To	Children's ministry director
Ministry Target	Children
Position Is	Volunteer
Position May Be Filled By	Church member
Minimum Maturity Level	Stable, maturing Christian
Spiritual Gifts	Pastor/shepherd • Administration • Exhortation
Talents or Abilities Desired	Ability to communicate well with others • Organizational and research skills
Best Personality Traits	Leader • Motivated • Analyst-dependable • Compassionate
Passion For	Involving children in home and foreign missions
Length of Service Commitment	One year minimum

ANTICIPATED TIME COMMITMENTS

1. **Doing ministry/preparing for ministry:** one to two hours a week
2. **Participating in meetings/training:** one hour a month

RESPONSIBILITIES/DUTIES

1. Research and remain aware of missions needs and opportunities.
2. Discover and approve curriculum or develop studies on missionaries to introduce children to missions: what it's all about, differences in culture, specific missionaries' lives. Arrange for missionaries to visit children's groups when possible.
3. Oversee children's missions study program.
4. Recruit and train missions study teachers and keep them informed.
5. Promote spiritual growth and concern for missions.

MISSIONS STUDY TEACHER

The missions study teacher is responsible for leading and teaching a group of children in missions awareness, study and involvement.

Ministry Area/Department	Children's ministry
Position	Missions study teacher
Accountable To	Missions study director
Ministry Target	Children
Position Is	Volunteer
Position May Be Filled By	Church member
Minimum Maturity Level	Stable, maturing Christian
Spiritual Gifts	Shepherding • Exhortation • Giving
Talents or Abilities Desired	Ability to communicate well with children
Best Personality Traits	Dependable • Motivated • Kindhearted
Passion For	Educating and involving children about home and foreign missions
Length of Service Commitment	One year minimum

ANTICIPATED TIME COMMITMENTS

1. **Doing ministry/preparing for ministry:** one to two hours a week
2. **Participating in meetings/training:** one hour a month

RESPONSIBILITIES/DUTIES

1. Work with missions study director to become aware of missions needs and opportunities.
2. Teach children about missions: what it's all about, differences in culture, specific missionary stories, etc. Missions study director will provide curriculum and arrange for missionaries to visit children's groups when possible.
3. Plan special missions projects for children. For example, adopt a missionary to correspond with and encourage, to send care packages to, etc.
4. Promote spiritual growth and concern for missions among children.

MISSIONS STUDY TEACHER ASSISTANT

The missions study teacher assistant is the missions study teacher's right hand. The assistant is responsible to provide support to the teacher and children and help keep order in the class during missions studies.

Ministry Area/Department	Children's ministry
Position	Missions study teacher assistant
Accountable To	Missions study teacher
Ministry Target	Children (ages 5 to 11)
Position Is	Volunteer
Position May Be Filled By	Church member
Minimum Maturity Level	New, growing Christian
Spiritual Gifts	Pastor/shepherd • Serving
Talents or Abilities Desired	Ability to communicate well with children and serve as a support person (for other leaders)
Best Personality Traits	Dependable • Motivated • Kindhearted
Passion For	Involving children in home and foreign missions and providing teacher support
Length of Service Commitment	One year minimum

ANTICIPATED TIME COMMITMENTS

1. **Doing ministry/preparing for ministry**: one hour a week
2. **Participating in meetings/training**: yearly training session

RESPONSIBILITIES/DUTIES

1. Work with missions study teacher to become aware of class plans.
2. Assist teacher as needed: prepare/distribute handouts, obtain supplies for class, etc.
3. Help children with special projects in class.
4. Escort younger children to the restroom or water fountain to insure safety and proper sanitation/hand washing.
5. Promote spiritual growth and concern for missions among children.

PRESCHOOL CLASS SECRETARY

The preschool class secretary is responsible for keeping accurate, up-to-date records; seeing that appropriate forms are completed regarding enrollment changes, visitors, etc.; preparing or assisting with class correspondence when needed and welcoming students to the class.

Ministry Area/Department	Children's Sunday School
Position	Preschool class secretary
Accountable To	Preschool teacher
Ministry Target	Children (ages 2 to 5/prekindergarten)
Position Is	Volunteer
Position May Be Filled By	Church member
Minimum Maturity Level	New, growing Christian
Spiritual Gifts	Administration • Serving
Talents or Abilities Desired	Good organizational skills • Attention to detail • Good penmanship
Best Personality Traits	Dependable-analyst • Cheerful
Passion For	Organization, accuracy and serving as a support person and must like children
Length of Service Commitment	One year minimum

ANTICIPATED TIME COMMITMENTS

1. **Doing ministry/preparing for ministry:** one hour a week
2. **Participating in meetings/training:** yearly training workshop

RESPONSIBILITIES/DUTIES

1. Participate in training opportunities yearly, or as presented.
2. Keep accurate records of attendance and up-to-date personal information (address, phone, birthday, etc.).
3. Welcome visitors, help new members feel accepted and greet all attendees.
4. Prepare name tags for preschoolers as they arrive.
5. Register visitors, obtaining names, addresses, phone numbers and parent names from the adults who bring children and determine whether or not families are members of another church.
6. Keep record of visitor and prospect information for outreach purposes. Have this information readily available to the teacher, outreach leader or other concerned staff.

7. Complete weekly attendance form, collect class offerings and turn them in to children's ministry records clerk.

8. Prepare or assist with special correspondence to class members.

PRESCHOOL EXTENDED SESSION DIRECTOR

The preschool extended session director is responsible for organizing and overseeing the preschool extended session program to insure proper leadership and exciting weekly sessions where young children can be taught principles from God's Word while having fun.

Ministry Area/Department	Children's ministry
Position	Preschool extended session director
Accountable To	Children's ministry director
Ministry Target	Preschoolers (ages 2 to 5/prekindergarten)
Position Is	Volunteer
Position May Be Filled By	Church member
Minimum Maturity Level	Stable, mature Christian
Spiritual Gifts	Exhortation • Pastor/shepherd • Administration
Talents or Abilities Desired	An enthusiastic speaker that relates well to children
Best Personality Traits	Cheerful • Energetic • Compassionate • Expresser-leader
Passion For	Influencing children's lives with God's love and message
Length of Service Commitment	One year minimum

ANTICIPATED TIME COMMITMENTS

1. Doing ministry/preparing for ministry: two-and-a-half hours a week
2. Participating in meetings/training: one hour a month

RESPONSIBILITIES/DUTIES

1. Participate in training opportunities yearly, or as presented.
2. Work with appropriate church staff or volunteers to construct or obtain props or materials needed for the children's extended session—held during adult worship service.
3. Recruit and train teachers and assistants for extended session.
4. Plan and organize weekly preschool extended-session program.
5. Coordinate with special speakers, puppeteers, musicians and any other ministers who will take part in the extended sessions.
6. Pray regularly for children and workers.
7. Work with children's ministry director to select or develop the curriculum for preschool extended sessions.
8. Oversee budget and expenditures for the preschool extended-session program.

PRESCHOOL EXTENDED SESSION TEACHER

The preschool extended session teacher is the shepherd of the class and is responsible to keep watch over the flock and oversee or coordinate all class leaders and functions. The teacher is expected to teach, reach and minister to members and prospects with the help of other leaders within the class.

Ministry Area/Department	Children's ministry
Position	Preschool extended session teacher
Accountable To	Preschool extended session director
Ministry Target	Preschoolers (prekindergarten/ages 2 to 5)
Position Is	Volunteer
Position May Be Filled By	Church member
Minimum Maturity Level	Stable, maturing Christian
Spiritual Gifts	Shepherding • Teaching • Exhortation
Talents or Abilities Desired	Ability to communicate well with children
Best Personality Traits	Dependable • Compassionate
Passion For	Nurturing a group of children • Teaching and leading them to Jesus
Length of Service Commitment	One year minimum

ANTICIPATED TIME COMMITMENTS

1. **Doing ministry/preparing for ministry:** two to three hours a week
2. **Participating in meetings/training:** one hour a month

RESPONSIBILITIES/DUTIES

1. Participate in teachers' meetings and training opportunities.
2. Work with the director to choose curriculum for your class.
3. Study and prepare for weekly lessons and activities. Gather necessary materials: handouts, craft supplies, etc.
4. Pray for class members and visitors.
5. Arrive 15 minutes before class begins to make sure classroom is prepared and to greet people as they arrive.
6. Lead class each week, involving children in studying and learning God's Word through various teaching methods and activities.
7. Promote spiritual growth and unity among class members.
8. Maintain contact with children and parents. Keep parents informed of topics/themes being studied, special events, etc. through printed notices, postcards and calls. Call, visit or send cards to students on special occasions or when a student is sick; class secretary can assist with these duties also.

PRESCHOOL EXTENDED SESSION TEACHER ASSISTANT

The preschool extended session assistant is the right arm of the preschool extended session teacher. The assistant must be prepared to fill in for the teacher when necessary and assist with keeping watch over the flock and coordinating class functions. The assistant is expected to teach, reach and minister to members and prospects under the direction of the teacher.

Ministry Area/Department	Children's ministry
Position	Preschool extended session teacher
Accountable To	Preschool extended session director
Ministry Target	Preschoolers (prekindergarten/ages 2 to 5)
Position Is	Volunteer
Position May Be Filled By	Church member
Minimum Maturity Level	Stable, maturing Christian
Spiritual Gifts	Shepherding • Teaching • Exhortation
Talents or Abilities Desired	Ability to communicate well with children
Best Personality Traits	Dependable • Compassionate
Passion For	Nurturing a group of children • Teaching and leading them to Jesus
Length of Service Commitment	One year minimum

ANTICIPATED TIME COMMITMENTS

1. **Doing ministry/preparing for ministry:** two hours a week
2. **Participating in meetings/training:** one hour a month

RESPONSIBILITIES/DUTIES

1. Participate in teacher's meetings and training opportunities.
2. Study each weekly lesson and be available to lead the class in the teacher's absence.
3. Assist teacher with preparing materials for class: handouts, craft supplies, etc.
4. Distribute handouts to children; help children with crafts or activities as needed.
5. Escort children to the restroom if it is not connected to the classroom. Assist younger children as needed; ensure hand washing. **Note:** It might be best if a woman is responsible for this task.
6. Pray for class members and visitors.
7. Promote spiritual growth and unity among class members.

PRESCHOOL SUNDAY SCHOOL TEACHER

The preschool teacher is the shepherd of the class and is responsible to keep watch over the flock and oversee or coordinate all class leaders and functions. The teacher is expected to teach, reach and minister to preschoolers with the help of other leaders within the class.

Ministry Area/Department	Children's Sunday School
Position	Preschool children's teacher
Accountable To	Children's ministry director (or Sunday School director, depending on church structure)
Ministry Target	Preschoolers (ages 2 to 5/prekindergarten)
Position Is	Volunteer
Position May Be Filled By	Church member
Minimum Maturity Level	Stable, maturing Christian
Spiritual Gifts	Shepherding • Teaching • Exhortation
Talents or Abilities Desired	Ability to communicate well with children
Best Personality Traits	Dependable-leader or expresser-leader • Compassionate
Passion For	Nurturing a group of children • Teaching and leading them to Jesus
Length of Service Commitment	One year minimum

ANTICIPATED TIME COMMITMENTS

1. **Doing ministry/preparing for ministry:** three hours a week
2. **Participating in meetings/training:** one hour a month

RESPONSIBILITIES/DUTIES

1. Participate in teachers' meetings and training opportunities.
2. Work with the director to choose curriculum for your class.
3. Study and prepare for weekly lessons and activities. Gather necessary materials: handouts, craft supplies, etc.
4. Pray for class members and visitors.
5. Arrive 15 minutes before class begins to make sure classroom is prepared and to greet children as they arrive.
6. Lead each week's class and involve children in studying and learning God's Word through various teaching methods and activities.
7. Plan and allow structured play activities in addition to the teaching.
8. Serve a light snack, such as crackers and juice, near the end of class period.

9. Maintain contact with children and parents. Keep parents informed of topics/themes being studied, special events, etc. through printed notices, postcards and calls. Call, visit or send cards to students on special occasions or when a student is sick; preschool class secretary can assist with these duties also.

PRESCHOOL SUNDAY SCHOOL TEACHER ASSISTANT

The preschool teacher assistant is the right arm of the preschool teacher. The assistant must be prepared to fill in for the teacher when necessary and assist with keeping watch over the flock and coordinating class functions. The assistant is expected to teach, reach and minister to the preschoolers under the direction of the teacher.

Ministry Area/Department	Children's Sunday School
Position	Preschool teacher assistant
Accountable To	Preschool teacher
Ministry Target	Preschoolers (prekindergarten/ages 2 to 5)
Position Is	Volunteer
Position May Be Filled By	Church member
Minimum Maturity Level	New, growing Christian
Spiritual Gifts	Shepherding • Serving • Exhortation
Talents or Abilities Desired	Able to communicate well with children • Able to allow someone else to lead, but willing to take the lead when necessary
Best Personality Traits	Dependable-expresser
Passion For	Discipling children and providing support for other leaders
Length of Service Commitment	One year minimum

ANTICIPATED TIME COMMITMENTS

1. **Doing ministry/preparing for ministry:** two hours a week
2. **Participating in meetings/training:** one hour a month

RESPONSIBILITIES/DUTIES

1. Participate in teachers' meetings and training opportunities.
2. Study each weekly lesson and be available to lead the class in the teacher's absence.
3. Assist teacher with preparing materials for class: handouts, craft supplies, etc.
4. Distribute handouts to children; help children with crafts or activities as needed.
5. Escort children to the restroom if it is not connected to the classroom. Assist younger children as needed; ensure hand washing. **Note:** It might be best if a woman is responsible for this task.
6. Help prepare and serve light snacks, such as crackers and juice, near end of class.
7. Pray for class members/visitors.

PUPPET DIRECTOR

The puppet director is responsible to oversee the entire puppet ministry and ensure excellence in organization, skit content and presentation. This arm of ministry will hold children's interest while helping them comprehend and retain God's Word.

Ministry Area/Department	Children's ministry
Position	Puppet director
Accountable To	Children's ministry director
Ministry Target	Preschoolers, children and occasionally other special groups
Position Is	Volunteer
Position May Be Filled By	Church member
Minimum Maturity Level	Stable, maturing Christian
Spiritual Gifts	Administration • Exhortation
Talents or Abilities Desired	Good organizational skills
Best Personality Traits	Dependable
Passion For	Discipling children through a creative puppet ministry
Length of Service Commitment	One year minimum

ANTICIPATED TIME COMMITMENTS

1. **Doing ministry/preparing for ministry**: two to three hours a week
2. **Participating in meetings/training**: one hour a month

RESPONSIBILITIES/DUTIES

1. Participate in leaders' meetings and training opportunities.
2. Recruit, train and organize puppeteers.
3. Plan and implement puppeteer rotation schedule.
4. Select or create puppet scripts.
5. Arrange to order or have puppets made and kept in good repair.
6. Contact volunteers to help construct props needed for the puppet ministry.
7. Direct rehearsals and presentations.
8. Schedule occasional special presentations for regular worship services, nursing homes, orphanages or other avenues of outreach.
9. Oversee budget and expenditures for the puppet ministry.

PUPPETEER

Puppeteers are responsible to prepare for and present weekly and special puppet presentations for the purpose of reaching and ministering to children or other special audiences.

Ministry Area/Department	Children's ministry
Position	Puppeteer
Accountable To	Puppet director
Ministry Target	Preschoolers, children and other special groups
Position Is	Volunteer
Position May Be Filled By	Regular attendee
Minimum Maturity Level	New, growing Christian
Spiritual Gifts	Serving • Exhortation
Talents or Abilities Desired	Organizational skills
Best Personality Traits	Dependable
Passion For	Puppetry and teaching children
Length of Service Commitment	One year minimum

ANTICIPATED TIME COMMITMENTS

1. **Doing ministry/preparing for ministry:** two to three hours a week
2. **Participating in meetings/training:** one hour a month

RESPONSIBILITIES/DUTIES

1. Participate in training sessions.
2. Study and rehearse puppet scripts.
3. Report puppet repair needs to puppet director.
4. Participate in puppet presentations.
5. Pray for the audience members prior to every presentation.

RESOURCE ROOM MANAGER

The resource room manager is responsible for managing the supplies and equipment available for children's ministry functions.

Ministry Area/Department	Children's ministry
Position	Resource room manager
Accountable To	Children's ministry director
Ministry Target	Preschool and children's teachers and assistants
Position Is	Volunteer
Position May Be Filled By	Church member
Minimum Maturity Level	New, growing Christian
Spiritual Gifts	Serving • Administration
Talents or Abilities Desired	Organizational skills
Best Personality Traits	Dependable • Team spirit • Leader-analyst or dependable-analyst
Passion For	Organization and efficiency • Providing support services to leaders
Length of Service Commitment	One year minimum

ANTICIPATED TIME COMMITMENTS

1. **Doing ministry/preparing for ministry:** one to two hours a week
2. **Participating in meetings/training:** no requirement

RESPONSIBILITIES/DUTIES

1. Organize and keep inventory record of supplies in the children's ministry resource room.
2. Report low inventory or special supply needs to children's ministry director.
3. Distribute supplies as needed to teachers; note items and quantity of inventory reduction on inventory record.
4. Sign out special equipment loaned to teachers and assistants. Sign in equipment returned.

VACATION BIBLE SCHOOL ASSISTANT

The Vacation Bible School (VBS) assistant is responsible for providing hands-on assistance in a designated area of VBS and helping keep order among the children throughout the program.

Ministry Area/Department	Children's ministry
Position	Vacation Bible School assistant
Accountable To	Vacation Bible School director
Ministry Target	Children of church members and unchurched neighbors
Position Is	Volunteer
Position May Be Filled By	Church member
Minimum Maturity Level	New, growing Christian
Spiritual Gifts	Serving • Shepherding
Talents or Abilities Desired	Communicate well with children
Best Personality Traits	Outgoing • Compassionate • Expresser-dependable or dependable-expresser
Passion For	Reaching children with God's love
Length of Service Commitment	One season

ANTICIPATED TIME COMMITMENTS

1. **Doing ministry/preparing for ministry**: four hours a day during VBS
2. **Participating in meetings/training**: two hours minimum planning and training prior to VBS

RESPONSIBILITIES/DUTIES

1. Assist VBS director or leader as needed in study, craft, game, special activity, music or refreshment sessions.
2. Help keep order; guide, direct or escort children to next activity, session or to restroom.

VACATION BIBLE SCHOOL DIRECTOR

The Vacation Bible School (VBS) director is responsible for planning, promoting and overseeing the entire VBS program.

Ministry Area/Department	Children's ministry
Position	Vacation Bible School director
Accountable To	Children's ministry director
Ministry Target	Children of church members and unchurched neighbors
Position Is	Volunteer
Position May Be Filled By	Church member
Minimum Maturity Level	Stable, maturing Christian
Spiritual Gifts	Administration • Shepherding • Exhortation
Talents or Abilities Desired	Good organizational and communication skills
Best Personality Traits	Dependable • Team Spirit • Motivator
Passion For	Reaching children with God's love
Length of Service Commitment	One season

ANTICIPATED TIME COMMITMENTS

1. **Doing ministry/preparing for ministry**: six hours a day during VBS
2. **Participating in meetings/training**: thirty hours in planning and organizing and in training workers during the two to three months prior to VBS

RESPONSIBILITIES/DUTIES

1. Coordinate with children's ministry director to order VBS curriculum and material.
2. Ensure that sufficient quantities of VBS supplies are available. Obtain craft materials, etc. through announcements for donations from church members. Purchase what is needed after donations.
3. Work with pastor and children's ministry director to recruit VBS workers.
4. Manage VBS promotion and registration.
5. Plan, promote and carry out a VBS worker-training workshop.
6. Distribute supplies to VBS workers.
7. Oversee entire VBS program; plan and direct special services/programs.
8. Collect visitor information from registration forms for follow-up:
   a. VBS director sends letter to children's parents, thanking them for allowing child to participate and inviting them to other church functions.
   b. Teachers send cards to students—thank-you-hope-you-enjoyed-come-again card.
   c. Give unchurched prospect information to church outreach director for follow-up.

9. Pray diligently for workers and children.
10. Oversee budget and expenditures for the VBS program.

VACATION BIBLE SCHOOL LEADER

The Vacation Bible School (VBS) leader is responsible to share God's love and teach His Word to children through a variety of methods, according to the area of ministry to which he or she is assigned.

Ministry Area/Department	Children's ministry
Position	Vacation Bible School leader
Accountable To	Vacation Bible School director
Ministry Target	Children of church members and unchurched neighbors
Position Is	Volunteer
Position May Be Filled By	Church member
Minimum Maturity Level	Stable, maturing Christian
Spiritual Gifts	Teaching • Exhortation • Shepherding
Talents or Abilities Desired	Communicate well with children
Best Personality Traits	Dependable-expresser or dependable-leader • Compassionate
Passion For	Reaching children with God's love
Length of Service Commitment	One season

ANTICIPATED TIME COMMITMENTS

1. **Doing ministry/preparing for ministry:** five hours a day during VBS
2. **Participating in meetings/training:** fifteen hours minimum planning and training prior to VBS

RESPONSIBILITIES/DUTIES

1. Provide leadership and instruction to a specific age-group of children in a designated area of VBS. Each leader will be assigned a specific area—teaching, craft-making, games, special activities, song leading, preparing/serving refreshments, etc.—to lead based on interests, experience, abilities and program needs.
2. Make sure supplies are available; work with assistants to prepare materials as needed for your area of ministry.
3. Study and prepare yourself to lead the children in your area of ministry.
4. Decorate, set up or otherwise prepare the room or space allowed for your area of ministry.
5. Pray for VBS program and specifically for workers and children.
6. Teachers mail thank-you cards to children to show appreciation for their participation in VBS and to encourage them to come again.

CREATIVE ARTS

ACTOR/ACTRESS

Actors and actresses are responsible to prepare for presenting God's Word through drama for the purpose of reaching people for Him and making a positive, life-changing impact on the audience. Actors and actresses will present skits to reinforce the pastor's message or to teach a Christian principle not necessarily associated with a specific message. Actors and actresses will also participate in special plays and seasonal dramatic events or musicals planned for evangelistic purposes.

Ministry Area/Department	Creative arts/drama
Position	Actor/actress
Accountable To	Drama team coordinator
Ministry Target	All ages of church members and occasional special community appearances
Position Is	Volunteer
Position May Be Filled By	Church member
Minimum Maturity Level	New, growing Christian
Spiritual Gifts	Serving
Talents or Abilities Desired	Able to perform in front of audiences and speak clearly • Interest in drama
Best Personality Traits	Expresser-dependable • Outgoing • Compassionate • Creative
Passion For	Using creative methods to share God's Word
Length of Service Commitment	One year minimum

ANTICIPATED TIME COMMITMENTS

1. **Doing ministry/preparing for ministry:** two hours a week—more for special performances
2. **Participating in meetings/training:** one hour a month

RESPONSIBILITIES/DUTIES

1. Participate in training sessions and planning meetings.
2. Study scripts and practice for upcoming skits or major drama presentations.
3. Meet with your drama team to rehearse your performance. Drama teams will serve on a rotating basis. How often you perform depends on how many drama teams are formed.
4. Be on time (or early), and do your best in performances as unto the Lord. If you are so ill you will not be able to perform, call your drama team coordinator or director immediately.
5. Before every performance, pray for God's anointing on the participants and for His Holy Spirit to prepare the hearts of those who will see and hear the performance.

BANNER BEARER

The banner bearer is responsible for glorifying the Lord through banner presentations in worship services or special events.

Ministry Area/Department	Creative arts/drama
Position	Banner bearer
Accountable To	Banner ministry coordinator
Ministry Target	Congregation in general
Position Is	Volunteer
Position May Be Filled By	Regular attendee
Minimum Maturity Level	New, growing Christian
Spiritual Gifts	Serving
Talents or Abilities Desired	Strong • Able to carry and hold banners (large or small, heavy or light) • Able to climb ladder when necessary to place banners where needed in the church
Best Personality Traits	Dependable-expresser or dependable-analyst
Passion For	Exalting the Lord • Decorating the house of the Lord to honor Him
Length of Service Commitment	One year minimum

ANTICIPATED TIME COMMITMENTS

1. **Doing ministry/preparing for ministry**: one hour a month—varies according to activities planned
2. **Participating in meetings/training**: a half hour a month—varies according to activities planned

RESPONSIBILITIES/DUTIES

1. Carry banners on special occasions during worship services or during special events such as Christmas musicals, Easter dramas, etc.
2. Place temporary or permanent banners where needed in church building—may require use of ladder or other equipment.
3. Participate in training or dress rehearsals for special events in which banners will be used.

BANNER DESIGNER/SEAMSTRESS

The banner designer/seamstress is responsible to assist in designing banners and making them for use in glorifying the Lord in worship services and special events.

Ministry Area/Department	Creative arts/drama
Position	Banner designer/seamstress
Accountable To	Banner ministry coordinator
Ministry Target	Congregation in general
Position Is	Volunteer
Position May Be Filled By	Regular attendee
Minimum Maturity Level	New, growing Christian
Spiritual Gifts	Serving
Talents or Abilities Desired	Craft-making and/or sewing experience • Able to do tedious, detailed work.
Best Personality Traits	Dependable • Hardworking • Analyst-dependable
Passion For	Using creative talent to exalt the Lord
Length of Service Commitment	One year minimum

ANTICIPATED TIME COMMITMENTS

1. **Doing ministry/preparing for ministry:** four hours a month—varies according to activities planned
2. **Participating in meetings/training:** a half hour a month—varies according to activities planned

RESPONSIBILITIES/DUTIES

1. Meet with banner ministry coordinator to discuss upcoming projects and deadlines.
2. Determine banner design based on needs of special project as shared by banner ministry coordinator.
3. Inform banner ministry coordinator of materials needed.
4. Work with other banner designers/seamstresses to carefully and prayerfully make banners as unto the Lord. This involves cutting patterns and material, sewing and or gluing, etc.
5. Repair banners as needed.

BANNER MINISTRY COORDINATOR

The banner ministry coordinator is responsible to coordinate with ministry leaders and direct volunteers to ensure an effective, well-organized ministry that uses banners in worshiping and glorifying the Lord.

Ministry Area/Department	Creative arts/drama
Position	Banner ministry coordinator
Accountable To	Pastor or pastor's designee
Ministry Target	Congregation in general
Position Is	Volunteer
Position May Be Filled By	Church member
Minimum Maturity Level	Stable, mature Christian
Spiritual Gifts	Administration • Exhortation
Talents or Abilities Desired	Organizational skills • Craft-making or sewing experience helpful
Best Personality Traits	Dependable • Leader-analyst
Passion For	Using creative talent to exalt the Lord
Length of Service Commitment	One year minimum

ANTICIPATED TIME COMMITMENTS

1. **Doing ministry/preparing for ministry**: one hour a month—varies according to activities planned
2. **Participating in meetings/training**: one hour a month—varies according to activities planned

RESPONSIBILITIES/DUTIES

1. Coordinate needs for banners with pastor, music director, drama director, etc.
2. Plan for new banner development as needed. Obtain materials needed.
3. Direct banner designers/seamstresses and banner bearers.
4. Maintain schedule for volunteers for banner design, making and repair.
5. Coordinate with appropriate ministry leaders and schedule banner bearers as needed for special events.
6. Oversee budget and expenditures for the banner ministry.

CHOREOGRAPHER

The choreographer is responsible for composing God-honoring choreography to complement special musicals or dramatic performances in or through the church and for teaching those movements to the participants.

Ministry Area/Department	Creative arts/drama
Position	Choreographer
Accountable To	Drama director
Ministry Target	All ages
Position Is	Volunteer
Position May Be Filled By	Church member
Minimum Maturity Level	New, growing Christian
Spiritual Gifts	Exhortation • Administration
Talents or Abilities Desired	Experience in choreography or creative movement/dance • Well-coordinated, with an ear for rhythm
Best Personality Traits	Outgoing • Energetic • Expresser-leader
Passion For	Glorifying God through tastefully arranged creative performances
Length of Service Commitment	One year minimum

ANTICIPATED TIME COMMITMENTS

1. **Doing ministry/preparing for ministry:** up to several hours a month, depending on timing of special performances
2. **Participating in meetings/training:** one hour a month—varies

RESPONSIBILITIES/DUTIES

1. Participate in training opportunities.
2. Coordinate with drama director, music director and creative dance ministry director to determine when choreography will be needed.
3. Design choreographic movements to complement special musicals: children, adults, seasonal, etc.
4. Teach choreography to dancers, choir members, actors/actresses or whoever will perform.
5. Oversee choreography in special performances.
6. Participate in practices/dress rehearsals as needed.

COSTUME CARETAKER

The costume caretaker is responsible to organize a costume closet, keep track of costumes and ensure that costumes are kept clean and in good repair.

Ministry Area/Department	Creative arts/drama
Position	Costume caretaker
Accountable To	Drama ministry director
Ministry Target	Participants in the creative arts/drama ministry
Position Is	Volunteer
Position May Be Filled By	Regular attendee
Minimum Maturity Level	New, growing Christian
Spiritual Gifts	Serving • Administration
Talents or Abilities Desired	Good organizational skills • Ability to determine laundering needs (wash or dry-clean)
Best Personality Traits	Dependable • Hardworking
Passion For	Cleanliness and orderliness
Length of Service Commitment	One year minimum

ANTICIPATED TIME COMMITMENTS

1. **Doing ministry/preparing for ministry**: up to eight hours a month—varies according to activities planned
2. **Participating in meetings/training**: an hour a month—varies according to activities planned

RESPONSIBILITIES/DUTIES

1. Meet with drama ministry director to keep abreast of upcoming projects and costume needs.
2. Organize a costume closet; keep a written inventory of costumes, sizes, etc.
3. Wash, dry and iron or send costumes to be dry-cleaned when necessary. Keep them in good condition and ready for use.
4. Contact a costume designer/seamstress when a costume needs repair and arrange to have repairs made.
5. Keep a sign-out/sign-in register for costumes to keep track of them at all times.
6. Oversee budget and expenditures for the costume ministry.

COSTUME DESIGNER/SEAMSTRESS

The costume designer/seamstress is responsible to create costumes to use in the church's drama ministry and to assist in keeping the costumes in good repair.

Ministry Area/Department	Creative arts/drama
Position	Costume designer/seamstress
Accountable To	Drama ministry director
Ministry Target	Participants in the creative arts/drama ministry
Position Is	Volunteer
Position May Be Filled By	Regular attendee
Minimum Maturity Level	New, growing Christian
Spiritual Gifts	Serving
Talents or Abilities Desired	Sewing experience • Able to do tedious, detailed work • Creative
Best Personality Traits	Dependable • Hardworking • Analyst-dependable
Passion For	Using creative talent to exalt the Lord
Length of Service Commitment	One year minimum

ANTICIPATED TIME COMMITMENTS

1. **Doing ministry/preparing for ministry**: zero to several hours a month—varies according to activities planned and number of costume designers/seamstresses involved
2. **Participating in meetings/training**: a half hour a month—varies according to activities planned

RESPONSIBILITIES/DUTIES

1. Meet with drama ministry director to discuss upcoming projects and deadlines.
2. Determine costume design based on needs of special project as shared by drama ministry director.
3. Obtain patterns and materials needed for costumes.
4. Work with other costume designers/seamstresses to carefully and prayerfully make costumes as unto the Lord. This involves cutting patterns and material, fitting and sewing, etc.
5. Repair costumes as needed.

CREATIVE DANCE MINISTRY DIRECTOR

The creative dance ministry director is responsible to plan and oversee a creative dance ministry that honors God and inspires the congregation.

Ministry Area/Department	Creative arts/drama
Position	Creative dance ministry director
Accountable To	Drama director
Ministry Target	All ages
Position Is	Volunteer
Position May Be Filled By	Church member
Minimum Maturity Level	Stable, maturing Christian
Spiritual Gifts	Exhortation • Administration
Talents or Abilities Desired	Experience in creative movement/dance preferred
Best Personality Traits	Outgoing • Energetic
Passion For	Glorifying God through tastefully arranged creative performances
Length of Service Commitment	One year minimum

ANTICIPATED TIME COMMITMENTS

1. **Doing ministry/preparing for ministry**: several hours a month, depending on timing of special performances
2. **Participating in meetings/training**: one hour a month—varies

RESPONSIBILITIES/DUTIES

1. Participate in training opportunities.
2. Coordinate with drama director and music director to plan creative dance presentations.
3. Work with choreographer when needed to develop special routines for musicals: children, adults, seasonal, etc.
4. Recruit, organize and oversee creative dancers involved in creative dance ministry, including ballet and creative/interpretive movement.
5. Participate in practices/dress rehearsals as needed.
6. Oversee budget and expenditures for the creative dance ministry.

CREATIVE DANCER

The creative dancer is responsible to perform beautiful creative dance that interprets special music or narrations and honors God.

Ministry Area/Department	Creative arts/drama
Position	Creative dancer
Accountable To	Creative dance ministry director
Ministry Target	All ages
Position Is	Volunteer
Position May Be Filled By	Regular attendee
Minimum Maturity Level	New, growing Christian
Spiritual Gifts	Exhortation • Serving
Talents or Abilities Desired	Experience in creative movement or ballet preferred
Best Personality Traits	Outgoing • Energetic • Expresser-dependable
Passion For	Interpreting music or message through dance and glorifying God through tastefully arranged creative performances
Length of Service Commitment	One year minimum

ANTICIPATED TIME COMMITMENTS

1. **Doing ministry/preparing for ministry:** up to ten hours a month, depending on timing of special performances
2. **Participating in meetings/training:** one hour a month—varies

RESPONSIBILITIES/DUTIES

1. Participate in training opportunities.
2. Work with creative dance ministry director and/or choreographer to develop interpretive routines for special musical or narrative presentations.
3. Participate in practices/dress rehearsals as needed.
4. Perform your ministry of dance to the Lord during worship services or special events as planned.

DECORATIONS ASSISTANT

The decorations assistant is responsible to assist the decorations coordinator in decorating to beautify the Lord's house and create environments that complement the current season, service or special event.

Ministry Area/Department	Creative arts/drama
Position	Decorations assistant
Accountable To	Decorations coordinator
Ministry Target	Congregation • All ages
Position Is	Volunteer
Position May Be Filled By	Church member
Minimum Maturity Level	New, growing Christian
Spiritual Gifts	Serving
Talents or Abilities Desired	Creative • Detail oriented
Best Personality Traits	Dependable • Cheerful • Cooperative spirit
Passion For	Beautifying the house of the Lord
Length of Service Commitment	One year minimum

ANTICIPATED TIME COMMITMENTS:

1. **Doing ministry/preparing for ministry**: up to ten hours a month
2. **Participating in meetings/training**: yearly training workshop

RESPONSIBILITIES/DUTIES

1. Assist decorations coordinator in obtaining, making and arranging decorations to use during special services, events or seasons.
2. Assist decorations coordinator in decorating the communion table, the foyer and sanctuary on a regular basis. This may include taking care of flower arrangements as needed, weekly, monthly or seasonally.
3. When requested, help decorate for special events such as fellowship meals, showers, receptions, banquets, seminars and so forth.
4. Assist with church bulletin board upkeep in common areas, but not in Sunday School rooms or areas under another ministry's jurisdiction.

DECORATIONS COORDINATOR

The decorations coordinator is responsible to organize and oversee church decorations as part of beautifying the Lord's house and creating environments that complement the current season, service or special event.

Ministry Area/Department	Creative arts/drama
Position	Decorations coordinator
Accountable To	Pastor
Ministry Target	Congregation • All ages
Position Is	Volunteer
Position May Be Filled By	Church member
Minimum Maturity Level	New, growing Christian
Spiritual Gifts	Administration, Serving
Talents or Abilities Desired	Good organizational skills • Attention to detail • Creative
Best Personality Traits	Dependable • Cheerful
Passion For	Sprucing up the house of the Lord
Length of Service Commitment	Two years minimum

ANTICIPATED TIME COMMITMENTS

1. **Doing ministry/preparing for ministry:** up to ten hours a month
2. **Participating in meetings/training:** yearly training workshop

RESPONSIBILITIES/DUTIES

1. Enlist decoration assistants and delegate tasks as necessary.
2. Obtain, make and arrange decorations to use during special services, events or seasons at the request of the pastor, music director, drama director or other ministry leader.
3. Decorate the Communion table, the foyer and sanctuary on a regular basis. Take care of flower arrangements as needed, weekly, monthly or seasonally.
4. When requested, decorate for special events such as fellowship meals, showers, receptions, banquets, seminars and so forth.
5. Supervise church bulletin boards in common areas, but not in Sunday School rooms or areas under another ministry's jurisdiction.
6. Organize and maintain a storage closet at the church for decorations and related supplies. This may include seasonal decorations, baby and wedding shower decorations, wedding supplies, anniversary decorations, etc.
7. Oversee budget and expenditures for the decorations ministry.

DRAMA DIRECTOR

The drama director is responsible for overseeing all aspects of the church drama ministry to ensure that presentations are as excellent and inspirational as possible.

Ministry Area/Department	Creative arts
Position	Drama director
Accountable To	Pastor (or pastor's designee)
Ministry Target	Congregation • Community in general
Position Is	Volunteer
Position May Be Filled By	Church member
Minimum Maturity Level	Stable, mature Christian
Spiritual Gifts	Exhortation • Pastor/shepherd • Administration
Talents or Abilities Desired	Leadership ability • Experience in drama a plus
Best Personality Traits	Detail oriented • Enthusiastic
Passion For	Presenting God's message through drama
Length of Service Commitment	Two years minimum

ANTICIPATED TIME COMMITMENTS

1. **Doing ministry/preparing for ministry**: up to ten hours a week, depending on drama productions scheduled
2. **Participating in meetings/training**: one hour a month

RESPONSIBILITIES/DUTIES

1. Oversee and pray for all aspects of the drama ministry.
2. Participate in training opportunities yearly, or as presented. Plan training sessions for drama ministry volunteers.
3. Research community for resources—libraries, fine arts centers, rental centers, colleges, bookstores, local theaters—to locate sources of props, costumes, etc. for drama presentations. Keep a log of suppliers and whether you rent, borrow or buy from them.
4. Look for new ideas and scripts to use in the church's drama ministry. Select scripts, or work with a creative writer within your church to write scripts, for skits, seasonal programs, plays, etc.
5. Recruit volunteers for drama ministry: actors, actresses, narrators, etc.
6. Work with appropriate church staff or volunteers to construct or obtain props or materials needed for drama productions.
7. Organize and schedule drama teams for skits, illustrated sermons, mimes, storytelling, clowning or whatever dramatic medium your church approves and has volunteers to carry out. Appoint a leader for each team.

8. Meet with banner ministry coordinator, choreographer, costume designers, creative dance ministry director and others to inform them of upcoming needs.

9. Oversee budget and expenditures for the drama ministry.

DRAMA TEAM LEADER

The drama team leader is responsible for overseeing and leading one drama team to insure meaningful presentations of skits, sermon illustrations or other drama medium—in worship services or other special events—as scheduled by the drama director.

Ministry Area/Department	Creative arts
Position	Drama team leader
Accountable To	Drama director
Ministry Target	Congregation • Community in general
Position Is	Volunteer
Position May Be Filled By	Church member
Minimum Maturity Level	Stable, mature Christian
Spiritual Gifts	Exhortation • Pastor/shepherd • Administration
Talents or Abilities Desired	Leadership ability • Experience in drama
Best Personality Traits	Detail oriented • Enthusiastic • Expresser-leader
Passion For	Presenting God's message through drama
Length of Service Commitment	One year minimum

ANTICIPATED TIME COMMITMENTS

1. **Doing ministry/preparing for ministry**: up to ten hours a week, depending on drama productions scheduled
2. **Participating in meetings/training**: one hour a month

RESPONSIBILITIES/DUTIES

1. Oversee, lead and pray for the drama team.
2. Participate in training opportunities yearly, or as presented.
3. Look for new ideas and scripts to use in your drama ministry. Work with drama director to select scripts for your team's skits, sermon illustrations, etc.
4. Recruit volunteers for your drama team.
5. Work with appropriate church staff or volunteers to construct or obtain props or materials needed for your team's drama productions.
6. Meet monthly with your drama team to discuss upcoming skits, sermon illustrations or other drama productions. Assign parts and duties. Set up rehearsals.
7. Inform drama director of any special needs.
8. Lead your drama team in presentations in worship services or other special occasions.

DRAMA TEAM MEMBER

The drama team member is responsible for rehearsing and working with other team members to present skits, sermon illustrations or other drama medium—in worship services or other special events—as scheduled by the drama team leader and director.

Ministry Area/Department	Creative arts
Position	Drama team member
Accountable To	Drama team leader
Ministry Target	Congregation • Community in general
Position Is	Volunteer
Position May Be Filled By	Regular attendee
Minimum Maturity Level	New, growing Christian
Spiritual Gifts	Exhortation • Serving
Talents or Abilities Desired	Interest in drama
Best Personality Traits	Creative • Expresser-dependable or expresser-leader
Passion For	Presenting God's message through drama
Length of Service Commitment	One year minimum

ANTICIPATED TIME COMMITMENTS

1. **Doing ministry/preparing for ministry:** three hours a week, depending on drama productions scheduled
2. **Participating in meetings/training:** one hour a month

RESPONSIBILITIES/DUTIES

1. Pray for the drama team.
2. Participate in training opportunities yearly, or as presented.
3. Study and memorize assigned scripts.
4. Rehearse skits.
5. Meet monthly with your drama team to discuss upcoming skits, sermon illustrations or other drama productions.
6. Perform drama presentation in worship services or other event.

NARRATOR

The narrator is responsible for rehearsing and working with other drama team members to deliver meaningful drama presentations—in worship services or other special events—as scheduled by the drama director.

Ministry Area/Department	Creative arts
Position	Narrator
Accountable To	Drama director
Ministry Target	Congregation • Community in general
Position Is	Volunteer
Position May Be Filled By	Regular attendee
Minimum Maturity Level	New, growing Christian
Spiritual Gifts	Exhortation • Serving
Talents or Abilities Desired	Interest in drama • Clear speech
Best Personality Traits	Expresser-analyst or expresser-dependable
Passion For	Presenting God's message through drama
Length of Service Commitment	One year minimum

ANTICIPATED TIME COMMITMENTS

1. **Doing ministry/preparing for ministry**: up to six hours a week, depending on drama productions scheduled
2. **Participating in meetings/training**: as called upon

RESPONSIBILITIES/DUTIES

1. Pray for your drama ministry.
2. Participate in training opportunities yearly, or as presented.
3. Participate in meetings as scheduled to learn about upcoming drama productions.
4. Study and memorize assigned scripts. Narrations may be read but are best when memorized.
5. Participate in rehearsals.
6. Deliver drama readings/narrations in drama presentations in worship services or other events.

SET DESIGN/CONSTRUCTION CREW LEADER

The set design/construction crew leader will coordinate with the drama director and oversee set construction and teardown for upcoming drama presentations.

Ministry Area/Department	Creative arts
Position	Set design/construction crew leader
Accountable To	Drama director
Ministry Target	Congregation • Community in general
Position Is	Volunteer
Position May Be Filled By	Church member
Minimum Maturity Level	New, growing Christian
Spiritual Gifts	Serving • Administration • Pastor/shepherd
Talents or Abilities Desired	Experience in construction work, preferably carpentry
Best Personality Traits	Dependable • Hardworking • Leader-analyst
Passion For	Contributing to the ministry through hands-on tasks and using expertise to enhance Christian drama presentations
Length of Service Commitment	One year minimum

ANTICIPATED TIME COMMITMENTS

1. **Doing ministry/preparing for ministry:** up to eight hours a week, depending on drama productions scheduled and props/staging needed
2. **Participating in meetings/training:** as called upon

RESPONSIBILITIES/DUTIES

1. Participate in meetings as scheduled to learn about upcoming drama productions.
2. Share input with drama director.
3. Gather construction materials as needed.
4. Call set design/construction crew members for assistance as needed.
5. Oversee design and construction of special staging, backdrops, props, etc. to ensure safe and attractive designs and timely completion, delivery and setup of finished materials.
6. Tear down and store special staging, backdrops, etc. after performances.

SET DESIGN/CONSTRUCTION CREW MEMBER

The set design/construction crew member will help construct sets for drama presentations.

Ministry Area/Department	Creative arts
Position	Set design/construction crew member
Accountable To	Set design/construction crew leader
Ministry Target	Congregation • Community in general
Position Is	Volunteer
Position May Be Filled By	Regular attendee
Minimum Maturity Level	New, growing Christian
Spiritual Gifts	Serving
Talents or Abilities Desired	Experience or ability in construction work preferred
Best Personality Traits	Dependable • Hardworking
Passion For	Contributing to the ministry through hands-on tasks and enhancing Christian drama presentations through top-quality set construction
Length of Service Commitment	One year minimum

ANTICIPATED TIME COMMITMENTS

1. **Doing ministry/preparing for ministry**: up to eight hours a week, depending on drama productions scheduled and props/staging needed
2. **Participating in meetings/training**: as called upon

RESPONSIBILITIES/DUTIES

1. Participate in meetings as scheduled to learn about upcoming drama productions.
2. Share input with leader.
3. Assist with construction of special staging, backdrops, props, etc. to ensure safe and attractive designs and timely completion, delivery and setup of finished materials.
4. Assist with tearing down and storing staging, backdrops, etc.

SET PAINTING ARTIST

The set painting artist will coordinate with the drama director and paint backdrops, props, etc. in preparation for special drama presentations.

Ministry Area/Department	Creative arts
Position	Set painting artist
Accountable To	Drama director
Ministry Target	Congregation • Community in general
Position Is	Volunteer
Position May Be Filled By	Regular attendee
Minimum Maturity Level	New, growing Christian
Spiritual Gifts	Serving
Talents or Abilities Desired	Artistic ability • Prefer experience in scenic painting
Best Personality Traits	Creative • Leader-dependable or leader-expresser
Passion For	Contributing to the ministry through hands-on tasks and using talent to enhance Christian drama presentations
Length of Service Commitment	One year minimum

ANTICIPATED TIME COMMITMENTS

1. **Doing ministry/preparing for ministry**: up to eight hours a week, depending on drama productions scheduled and props/staging needed
2. **Participating in meetings/training**: as called upon

RESPONSIBILITIES/DUTIES

1. Participate in meetings as scheduled to learn about upcoming drama productions.
2. Share input with drama director.
3. Obtain and maintain needed art supplies.
4. Coordinate with set design/construction crew leader as necessary.
5. Paint special backdrops, props, etc. to enhance drama presentations and lend to the desired atmosphere.

SPECIAL PRODUCTION DIRECTOR

The special production director is responsible for overseeing and directing major, special drama productions.

Ministry Area/Department	Creative arts
Position	Special production director
Accountable To	Drama director
Ministry Target	Congregation • Community in general
Position Is	Volunteer
Position May Be Filled By	Church member
Minimum Maturity Level	Stable, mature Christian
Spiritual Gifts	Administration • Pastor/shepherd
Talents or Abilities Desired	Experience in drama preferred • Leadership ability
Best Personality Trait	Dependable-leader or expresser-leader • Good communicator
Passion For	Glorifying God and influencing lives through meaningful drama presentations
Length of Service Commitment	One year minimum

ANTICIPATED TIME COMMITMENTS

1. **Doing ministry/preparing for ministry**: up to eight hours a week, depending on drama productions scheduled and props/staging needed
2. **Participating in meetings/training**: as called upon

RESPONSIBILITIES/DUTIES

1. Participate in meetings as scheduled to learn about upcoming drama productions.
2. Share input with drama director.
3. Study drama scripts to get a feel for the message, the atmosphere and how to present it.
4. Work with drama director to cast the parts using those who have volunteered as actors/actresses, narrators, drama team members, etc. If necessary, recruit other cast members.
5. Distribute copies of scripts to cast members.
6. Meet with all cast members to explain the goal of the drama presentation, the personalities each character should portray, your expectations of them and the rehearsal schedule.
7. Direct the rehearsals and make suggestions for ways to improve the presentations for maximum impact.
8. Meet with drama director to discuss needs for set construction, music, soloists, lighting, sound, dancers or other participants. Work with drama director to coordinate with other leaders regarding these needs.

THEATRICAL MAKEUP ARTIST

The theatrical makeup artist will use makeup to accentuate actors' and actresses' features and to make actors and actresses look like the characters they portray. The theatrical makeup artist will need to be familiar with the characters of the drama presentation in order to apply makeup most effectively. Makeup might not be necessary in skits done to reinforce the pastor's message or to teach a Christian principle; however, makeup will be necessary in special plays and seasonal dramatic events or musicals.

Ministry Area/Department	Creative arts/drama
Position	Theatrical makeup artist
Accountable To	Drama team coordinator or special production director
Ministry Target	Actors/actresses
Position Is	Volunteer
Position May Be Filled By	Regular attendee
Minimum Maturity Level	New, growing Christian
Spiritual Gifts	Serving
Talents or Abilities Desired	Knowledge of stage makeup preferred; however, any experience with makeup application is acceptable
Best Personality Trait	Gentle • Creative • Dependable-expresser or dependable-leader
Passion For	Helping actors/actresses look their parts in Christian drama
Length of Service Commitment	One year minimum

ANTICIPATED TIME COMMITMENTS

1. **Doing ministry/preparing for ministry:** one hour a week—more during special performances
2. **Participating in meetings/training:** one hour a month

RESPONSIBILITIES/DUTIES

1. Participate in training sessions and planning meetings.
2. Learn the characters for upcoming skits or major drama presentations.
3. Meet with the drama team to determine makeup needs.
4. Arrive early to allow plenty time to make up actors/actresses—30 minutes or more, depending on extent of your makeup services. If you are so ill you will not be able to assist, call your drama team coordinator or special production director immediately.

5. Before every performance, pray for God's anointing on the participants and for His Holy Spirit to prepare the hearts of those who will see and hear the performance.

6. Purchase makeup and related supplies as needed with approval from the drama director.

FAMILY

FAMILY LIFE PASTOR

The family life pastor is responsible for encouraging the growth of spiritually healthy families through providing leadership, pastoral care, outreach and educational services.

Ministry Area/Department	Family
Position	Family life pastor
Accountable To	Pastor
Ministry Target	Families • All ages
Position Is	Paid staff
Position May Be Filled By	Church member
Minimum Maturity Level	Solid, very mature Christian
Spiritual Gifts	Pastor/shepherd • Administration • Exhortation
Talents or Abilities Desired	Completed counseling courses, including some experience in counseling • Understanding of God's Word as it relates to family roles • Ability to care for a group of people and communicate well with others • Leadership potential/ability • Previous ministry experience preferred
Best Personality Traits	Compassionate • Dependable • Expresser-leader
Passion For	Strengthening and supporting the family
Length of Service Commitment	Two years minimum

ANTICIPATED TIME COMMITMENTS

1. **Doing ministry/preparing for ministry:** forty hours a week, off on Saturday and one day during week, except for emergencies and special occasions
2. **Participating in meetings/training:** one hour a month

RESPONSIBILITIES/DUTIES

1. Participate in staff/church planning meetings.
2. Regularly participate in church visitation:
   a. Make follow-up visits to families who have visited the church.
   b. Develop and carry out an organized plan to visit and build relationships with church families.
   c. Visit family members who do not attend church, such as parents of children or teens who attend. Purpose is to meet them and compliment their children, to build relationships, to inform them of church ministries and invite them to visit or become involved, to determine spiritual condition for future contacts.

3. Counsel and pray with families who are having difficulties with their family relationships or other family problems. Refer to a professional counselor when necessary.

4. Conduct premarital counseling to prepare couples for marriage and family life.

5. Lead classes on marriage, family relationships, parenting, caring for elderly parents and other pertinent subjects related to family. Invite guest speakers occasionally.

6. Plan special family activities periodically—perhaps a yearly family emphasis week full of special events, fun activities, seminars, etc.

7. Perform weddings, baby dedications, marriage renewal ceremonies, etc.

8. Oversee budget and expenditures for the family life ministry.

HOSPITALITY

FELLOWSHIP COORDINATOR

The fellowship coordinator is responsible for planning and coordinating churchwide fellowship activities. This person will recruit volunteers or contact appropriate ministry directors or committee members for assistance as needed.

Ministry Area/Department	Fellowship
Position	Fellowship coordinator
Accountable To	Pastor or executive pastor
Ministry Target	All ages
Position Is	Volunteer
Position May Be Filled By	Church member
Minimum Maturity Level	New, growing Christian
Spiritual Gifts	Administration • Exhortation • Serving
Talents or Abilities Desired	Good organizational skills • Enjoy dealing with people
Best Personality Traits	Friendly • Dependable-expresser or expresser-analyst
Passion For	Strengthening the Body of Christ through fellowship
Length of Service Commitment	One year minimum

ANTICIPATED TIME COMMITMENTS

1. **Doing ministry/preparing for ministry:** four hours a month
2. **Participating in meetings/training:** one hour a quarter

RESPONSIBILITIES/DUTIES

1. Plan, organize and oversee churchwide fellowship events no less than once a quarter. Events could include picnics, potlucks, ice cream socials, family sports days and skating parties.
2. Recruit volunteers or contact appropriate ministry directors to assist with food preparation/service, set up facilities, decorations, equipment needs, publicity, etc.

FOOD SERVICE ASSISTANT

The food service assistant is responsible for helping the food-service director prepare and/or serve meals served on church grounds and clean up afterward.

Ministry Area/Department	Fellowship
Position	Food service assistant
Accountable To	Food service director
Ministry Target	Congregation and guests
Position Is	Volunteer
Position May Be Filled By	Regular attendee
Minimum Maturity Level	New, growing Christian
Spiritual Gifts	Serving
Talents or Abilities Desired	Good cooking skills • Attention to cleanliness
Best Personality Traits	Very neat and clean • Cooperative • Hospitable • Dependable-leader or dependable-expresser
Passion For	Preparing meals and for serving people
Length of Service Commitment	One year minimum

ANTICIPATED TIME COMMITMENTS

1. **Doing ministry/preparing for ministry**: three hours a month (more if unable to rotate assistants)
2. **Participating in meetings/training**: minimal, as needed

RESPONSIBILITIES/DUTIES

1. Assist with food preparation and service for fellowship meals, special luncheons or dinners and any church-related meal held on the grounds.
2. May include one or more of the following: cook, grill, serve and clean up tables and dishes after meals.

FOOD SERVICE DIRECTOR

The food service director is responsible for planning and coordinating all meals served on church grounds. This includes working in conjunction with the fellowship coordinator when fellowship events involve meals.

Ministry Area/Department	Fellowship
Position	Food service director
Accountable To	Executive pastor
Ministry Target	Congregation and guests
Position Is	Volunteer
Position May Be Filled By	Church member
Minimum Maturity Level	New, growing Christian
Spiritual Gifts	Administration • Serving
Talents or Abilities Desired	Good organizational skills • Cooking skills, especially for large groups
Best Personality Traits	Very neat and clean • Dependable • Analyst-expresser
Passion For	Planning and preparing meals and for serving people
Length of Service Commitment	One year minimum

ANTICIPATED TIME COMMITMENTS

1. **Doing ministry/preparing for ministry:** three hours a week
2. **Participating in meetings/training:** minimal, as needed

RESPONSIBILITIES/DUTIES

1. Plan, organize and oversee food preparation and service for fellowship meals, special luncheons or dinners and any church-related meal held on the grounds.
2. Purchase any food/drinks/supplies to be furnished by the church.
3. Recruit assistants to help cook, grill, serve and clean up tables and dishes after meals.
4. Organize potlucks by assigning certain types of foods—such as meats, casseroles, salads, desserts, etc.—to different groups within the congregation, such as by classes, names beginning with certain letters of the alphabet, or by asking that each family bring a main dish and dessert or salad.
5. Oversee budget and expenditures for the food service ministry.

GREETER

The greeter is responsible to ensure that every person entering the church is greeted and that visitors are offered assistance as appropriate so that everyone feels important and welcome. Greeters will be asked to serve during special events also.

Ministry Area/Department	Hospitality
Position	Greeter
Accountable To	Hospitality coordinator
Ministry Target	Congregation and guests
Position Is	Volunteer
Position May Be Filled By	Church member
Minimum Maturity Level	New, growing Christian
Spiritual Gifts	Serving • Exhortation
Talents or Abilities Desired	Comfortable talking to/greeting guests • Able to give good directions regarding church facilities
Best Personality Traits	Hospitable, not shy (or able to overcome shyness) • Sensitive to needs and feelings of others • Dependable-expresser
Passion For	Making people feel welcome
Length of Service Commitment	One year minimum

ANTICIPATED TIME COMMITMENTS

1. **Doing ministry/preparing for ministry:** one hour a month—more during special events
2. **Participating in meetings/training:** minimal, as needed

RESPONSIBILITIES/DUTIES

1. Greet members and guests as they enter or exit the building.
2. Greet visitors at the welcome center and provide information as needed or requested.
3. Direct visitors to classes, nursery, sanctuary, restrooms, etc.
4. Introduce visitors to church staff, teachers and members of similar age when possible.
5. Open doors for/assist the elderly or disabled.

HOSPITALITY COORDINATOR

The hospitality coordinator will oversee the hospitality ministry to ensure that every person entering the church is greeted and that visitors are offered assistance as appropriate so that everyone feels important and welcome and is able to find his or her desired destination easily.

Ministry Area/Department	Hospitality
Position	Hospitality coordinator
Accountable To	Executive pastor
Ministry Target	Congregation and guests
Position Is	Volunteer
Position May Be Filled By	Church member
Minimum Maturity Level	New, growing Christian
Spiritual Gifts	Serving • Exhortation • Administration
Talents or Abilities Desired	Comfortable talking to and greeting guests • Ability to give good directions regarding church facilities • Ability to lead and direct others
Best Personality Traits	Hospitable • Outgoing • Sensitive to needs and feelings of others • Dependable-expresser or expresser-analyst
Passion For	Making people feel welcome
Length of Service Commitment	One year minimum

ANTICIPATED TIME COMMITMENTS

1. **Doing ministry/preparing for ministry**: one hour a week
2. **Participating in meetings/training**: minimal, as needed

RESPONSIBILITIES/DUTIES

1. Greet members and guests.
2. Direct or lead visitors to their desired destination.
3. Introduce visitors to church staff, teachers and members of similar age when possible.
4. Open doors for/assist the elderly or disabled.
5. Recruit and coordinate schedule of ushers and greeters to assist with welcoming and directing others on a regular basis as well as for special events. Maintain a list of greeters' phone numbers and addresses.
6. Oversee the welcome center operation.
7. Make sure the welcome center is stocked with information about the church's ministries, tracts, a map of the church, etc.

8. Recruit and coordinate schedule of parking lot attendants to assist with traffic flow, visitor and handicapped parking and directions for all church services and major events.

9. Oversee budget and expenditures for the hospitality ministry.

KITCHEN DIRECTOR

The kitchen director is responsible for organizing and overseeing the use of the church kitchen.

Ministry Area/Department	Hospitality/fellowship
Position	Kitchen director
Accountable To	Executive pastor
Ministry Target	Congregation and guests
Position Is	Volunteer
Position May Be Filled By	Church member
Minimum Maturity Level	New, growing Christian
Spiritual Gifts	Serving • Administration
Talents or Abilities Desired	Good organizational skills
Best Personality Traits	Dependable-leader • Hospitable
Passion For	Orderly and clean facilities to promote an efficient fellowship ministry
Length of Service Commitment	Two years minimum

ANTICIPATED TIME COMMITMENTS

1. **Doing ministry/preparing for ministry:** one to three hours a week
2. **Participating in meetings/training:** minimal, as needed

RESPONSIBILITIES/DUTIES

1. Supervise all activities using the church kitchen.
2. Keep an inventory list of kitchen supplies and equipment and request funds to replace, repair or add to the inventory when needed.
3. Organize and clean the kitchen and appliances as needed.
4. Establish and post policies for the use and care of the kitchen.
5. Keep a running list in the kitchen so that those who use the kitchen know when supplies are low or depleted.

PARKING LOT ATTENDANT

The parking lot attendant is an extension of the hospitality ministry and will help ensure that visitors and people in need are made to feel welcome and are offered appropriate assistance. This person will also help direct traffic when necessary.

Ministry Area/Department	Hospitality
Position	Parking lot attendant
Accountable To	Hospitality coordinator
Ministry Target	Congregation and guests
Position Is	Volunteer
Position May Be Filled By	Church member
Minimum Maturity Level	New, growing Christian
Spiritual Gifts	Serving
Talents or Abilities Desired	Physically able to direct and assist with traffic flow in any weather condition • Enjoy working outside • Able to present a positive image and assist the disabled with parking and church entry
Best Personality Traits	Dependable • Hospitable • Even tempered
Passion For	Serving and welcoming others
Length of Service Commitment	One year minimum

ANTICIPATED TIME COMMITMENTS

1. Doing ministry/preparing for ministry: one hour a week
2. Participating in meetings/training: minimal, as needed

RESPONSIBILITIES/DUTIES

1. Direct traffic and parking when crowd and traffic congestion warrants it.
2. Greet visitors in the parking lot and direct them to appropriate entrance.
3. Assist the elderly and disabled with church entry as needed.
4. Offer to provide an umbrella escort for elderly, disabled and visitors if it's raining.

RECEPTION SERVER

The reception server will assist the kitchen director or hostess by serving food and beverages at churchwide receptions and will display a gracious, friendly attitude.

Ministry Area/Department	Hospitality
Position	Reception server
Accountable To	Food service director
Ministry Target	Congregation • Guests
Position Is	Volunteer
Position May Be Filled By	Church member
Minimum Maturity Level	New, growing Christian
Spiritual Gifts	Serving
Talents or Abilities Desired	Physically able to serve refreshments • Enjoy meeting and serving others
Best Personality Traits	Dependable-expresser • Hospitable • Gracious
Passion For	For serving and welcoming others
Length of Service Commitment	One year minimum

ANTICIPATED TIME COMMITMENTS

1. **Doing ministry/preparing for ministry:** two hours a month or as needed
2. **Participating in meetings/training:** minimal, as needed

RESPONSIBILITIES/DUTIES

1. Assist in serving food and beverages at churchwide receptions for special guests, visitors, special events, baby and wedding showers for members.
2. Optional opportunity to assist in serving food and beverages at private receptions: weddings, anniversaries, etc.

USHER

The usher will regularly participate in worship services and will assist with literature distribution; welcoming, directing and seating guests and others as needed; and collecting offerings.

Ministry Area/Department	Hospitality
Position	Usher
Accountable To	Hospitality coordinator
Ministry Target	Congregation and guests
Position Is	Volunteer
Position May Be Filled By	Church member
Minimum Maturity Level	New, growing Christian
Spiritual Gifts	Serving
Talents or Abilities Desired	Able to stand for periods of time • Enjoy greeting and seating people.
Best Personality Traits	Dependable-leader or dependable-expresser • Hospitable • Gracious
Passion For	Serving and welcoming others
Length of Service Commitment	One year minimum

ANTICIPATED TIME COMMITMENTS

1. **Doing ministry/preparing for ministry**: one-and-a-half hours a week—may serve on a rotating schedule (e.g., every three months for a month or once every four weeks, etc.)
2. **Participating in meetings/training**: minimal, as needed

RESPONSIBILITIES/DUTIES

1. Attend worship services.
2. Watch for and welcome guests.
3. Assist guests and members and latecomers with seating as needed.
4. Distribute literature as called upon, such as visitor packets, bulletins, sermon outlines, tracts, etc.
5. Receive tithes and offerings and leave them with the appropriate person.
6. Offer directions when needed.
7. Open doors and assist elderly and disabled individuals as needed.

WELCOME CENTER GUIDE

The welcome center guide will display a gracious, friendly attitude in showing guests the church facilities and answering questions regarding the facilities and ministry locations. This person will portray the church in a positive image and will help guests feel welcome.

Ministry Area/Department	Hospitality
Position	Welcome center guide
Accountable To	Hospitality coordinator
Ministry Target	Guests
Position Is	Volunteer
Position May Be Filled By	Church member
Minimum Maturity Level	New, growing Christian
Spiritual Gifts	Serving
Talents or Abilities Desired	Knowledge of church facilities • Able to give good directions • Physically able to walk throughout the facilities and stand for periods of time
Best Personality Traits	Dependable-leader or dependable-expresser • Hospitable • Gracious
Passion For	Serving and welcoming others
Length of Service Commitment	One year minimum

ANTICIPATED TIME COMMITMENTS

1. **Doing ministry/preparing for ministry:** one hour a week
2. **Participating in meetings/training:** minimal, as needed

RESPONSIBILITIES/DUTIES

1. Guide guests through church facilities.
2. Answer questions regarding church facilities and locations of specific ministries.
3. Present a positive image of the church.
4. Distribute church literature as needed.

LIBRARY

BOOK PROCESSING ASSISTANT

The book processing assistant will help the librarian prepare and maintain books for inclusion in the church library.

Ministry Area/Department	Library
Position	Book processing assistant
Accountable To	Librarian
Ministry Target	All ages
Position Is	Volunteer
Position May Be Filled By	Church member
Minimum Maturity Level	New, growing Christian
Spiritual Gifts	Administration • Serving
Talents or Abilities Desired	Good organizational skills • Enjoy books and filing
Best Personality Traits	Analyst-dependable
Passion For	Maintaining a Christian resource center to edify the saints
Length of Service Commitment	One year minimum

ANTICIPATED TIME COMMITMENTS

1. **Doing ministry/preparing for ministry:** one to two hours a month
2. **Participating in meetings/training:** one hour a quarter

RESPONSIBILITIES/DUTIES

Assist librarian with assimilating new and used books into the church library:

a. Stamp church name and address inside.

b. Glue in envelope for checkout card, or attach other device used for tracking such as bar code.

c. File books in proper location on shelf after proper cataloging has been done by the librarian.

d. Repair torn pages or worn binding with tape.

BOOK REVIEWER

The book reviewer is responsible to review book content to make sure books are appropriate for the church library, to recommend new books for the library and to provide occasional reviews of new library books for the church newsletter.

Ministry Area/Department	Library
Position	Book reviewer
Accountable To	Librarian
Ministry Target	Congregation
Position Is	Volunteer
Position May Be Filled By	Church member
Minimum Maturity Level	Stable, mature Christian
Spiritual Gifts	Teaching • Discerning • Pastor/shepherd
Talents or Abilities Desired	A love of reading • Knowledge of basic doctrine and this church's views • Ability to review and criticize books
Best Personality Traits	Analyst-dependable • Discerning
Passion For	For reading and sharing knowledge with others
Length of Service Commitment	One year minimum

ANTICIPATED TIME COMMITMENTS

1. **Doing ministry/preparing for ministry**: three hours a week
2. **Participating in meetings/training**: minimal, as needed

RESPONSIBILITIES/DUTIES

1. Read and recommend books for the church library.
2. Review books donated to the library to ensure their appropriateness for the library.
3. Provide brief written reviews of new library books for the church newsletter.

DESK CLERK

The desk clerk will be available as scheduled to assist with book checkout and returns and to direct people to the sections they are trying to locate.

Ministry Area/Department	Library
Position	Desk clerk
Accountable To	Librarian
Ministry Target	Congregation
Position Is	Volunteer
Position May Be Filled By	Church member or other approved individual
Minimum Maturity Level	New, growing Christian
Spiritual Gifts	Serving
Talents or Abilities Desired	Good organizational skills
Best Personality Traits	Organized • Dependable-expresser • Friendly
Passion For	Assisting others • Growing spiritually through Christian resources
Length of Service Commitment	One year minimum

ANTICIPATED TIME COMMITMENTS

1. **Doing ministry/preparing for ministry:** one hour a week
2. **Participating in meetings/training:** minimal, as needed

RESPONSIBILITIES/DUTIES

1. Be available at the library desk to assist with book checkout.
2. Receive and check in book returns.
3. Be familiar with book topics in library and direct people to sections for which they are searching.

HISTORIAN

The historian is responsible for keeping accurate records and photos of church events and milestones and organizing the information to preserve a historical library of the church's heritage.

Ministry Area/Department	Library
Position	Historian
Accountable To	Church board
Ministry Target	Congregation
Position Is	Volunteer
Position May Be Filled By	Church member
Minimum Maturity Level	Stable, maturing Christian
Spiritual Gifts	Administration • Serving
Talents or Abilities Desired	Good research and organizational skills • Very neat • Detail oriented
Best Personality Traits	Analyst-dependable or analyst-expresser
Passion For	Preserving a record of the church's history and accomplishments
Length of Service Commitment	Indefinite

ANTICIPATED TIME COMMITMENTS

1. **Doing ministry/preparing for ministry:** one hour a month—occasionally more
2. **Participating in meetings/training:** minimal, as needed

RESPONSIBILITIES/DUTIES

1. Clip and file any news or magazine articles about the church, pastor or related ministries.
2. Keep photo archives by properly identifying photos of:
   a. All pastors and paid staff members who have served the church;
   b. Special events;
   c. Church building, grounds and any additions or improvements.
3. Keep an up-to-date journal about any special services and events held at the church: revivals, homecomings, anniversaries, dramas, ministry fairs, etc.
4. Keep a record of church expansions and improvements; note dates, etc.
5. Keep up-to-date biographical information about the pastor(s).
6. Take photos of special people and events, or arrange for someone else to do so.
7. File a copy of every church yearbook that is created.

LIBRARIAN

The librarian is responsible for organizing and maintaining the church library.

Ministry Area/Department	Library
Position	Librarian
Accountable To	Executive pastor
Ministry Target	Congregation
Position Is	Volunteer
Position May Be Filled By	Church member
Minimum Maturity Level	Stable, maturing Christian
Spiritual Gifts	Serving • Exhortation • Administration
Talents or Abilities Desired	Strong organizational skills • Experience in library work helpful • Able to type and write legibly • Detail oriented
Best Personality Traits	Analyst-expresser or analyst-dependable
Passion For	Helping others grow spiritually through printed and audiovisual resources
Length of Service Commitment	Two years minimum

ANTICIPATED TIME COMMITMENTS

1. **Doing ministry/preparing for ministry:** two to three hours a week
2. **Participating in meetings/training:** minimal, as needed

RESPONSIBILITIES/DUTIES

1. Schedule, coordinate and oversee library assistants and book reviewers.
2. Obtain new and used books for library. Work with reviewers to seek approval, comments and recommendations.
3. Catalog and prepare all books for inclusion in the library:
   a. Stamp church name/address inside.
   b. Prepare for checkout with envelope or card in back or bar code or other tracking method.
   c. File books in proper location after cataloging.
4. Repair torn pages/weak bindings before shelving books.
5. Oversee book checkout and return.
6. Shelve books in proper location.
7. Assist others with locating specific books/topics.
8. Follow up on overdue books.
9. Oversee budget and expenditures for the library.

YEARBOOK ASSISTANT

The yearbook assistant will help organize and ensure efficiency and accuracy during photo sessions.

Ministry Area/Department	Library
Position	Yearbook assistant
Accountable To	Yearbook coordinator
Ministry Target	Congregation
Position Is	Volunteer
Position May Be Filled By	Church member
Minimum Maturity Level	New, growing Christian
Spiritual Gifts	Administration • Serving
Talents or Abilities Desired	Good spelling and organizational skills • Desire to assist others • Detail oriented
Best Personality Traits	Expresser-analyst or dependable-expresser
Passion For	Accuracy and excellence
Length of Service Commitment	One year

ANTICIPATED TIME COMMITMENTS

1. **Doing ministry/preparing for ministry**: four to eight hours a week for one month or more, depending on church size
2. **Participating in meetings/training**: minimal, as needed

RESPONSIBILITIES/DUTIES

1. Follow schedule and double-check names, spelling, etc. during photo sessions.
2. Assist members as needed when preparing for photo sessions.
3. Call appointments who are late to try to determine if they are coming or to reschedule.

YEARBOOK COORDINATOR

The yearbook coordinator is responsible for overseeing the planning and production of the church yearbook.

Ministry Area/Department	Library
Position	Yearbook coordinator
Accountable To	Executive pastor
Ministry Target	Congregation
Position Is	Volunteer
Position May Be Filled By	Church member
Minimum Maturity Level	New, growing Christian
Spiritual Gifts	Administration
Talents or Abilities Desired	Excellent organizational skills • Detail oriented
Best Personality Traits	Leader-dependable
Passion For	Producing a complete and accurate yearbook of church members
Length of Service Commitment	One year

ANTICIPATED TIME COMMITMENTS

1. **Doing ministry/preparing for ministry:** approximately sixty hours or more during one quarter of one year, depending upon church size
2. **Participating in meetings/training:** minimal, as needed

RESPONSIBILITIES/DUTIES

1. Obtain quotes from photography studios to come to the church for photo sessions and do yearbook printing.
2. Schedule dates and times for photographer to come to church and coordinate details.
3. Prepare sign-up sheets for congregation.
4. Recruit assistants to help follow schedule and double check names/spelling, etc. during photo sessions.
5. Make sure church is open during sessions.
6. Put reminder in church bulletins/newsletter for at least two weeks before photo sessions.
7. Oversee yearbook cover design or photo selection for cover.
8. Obtain any special photographs to be included in the yearbook and give them to the photographer or appropriate person.
9. Finalize details with photographer and follow through until the yearbook is complete and has been printed.
10. Oversee budget and expenditures for the church yearbook.

MEDIA

AUDIO TECHNICIAN

The audio technician will record messages and special music presented during regular church worship services and occasional special services; keep an organized library of tape recordings; provide duplicate audiocassette tapes for the tape ministry, which provides recordings for people who are unable to attend services or who desire to share messages with others.

Ministry Area/Department	Media
Position	Audio technician
Accountable To	Executive pastor
Ministry Target	Congregation • Community
Position Is	Volunteer
Position May Be Filled By	Church member
Minimum Maturity Level	New, growing Christian
Spiritual Gifts	Serving
Talents or Abilities Desired	Training and/or experience in operating sound recording equipment • Good hearing
Best Personality Traits	Dependable • Consistent • Leader-analyst or dependable-analyst
Passion For	Professionally recording messages and music for the glory of God
Length of Service Commitment	One year minimum

ANTICIPATED TIME COMMITMENTS

1. **Doing ministry/preparing for ministry**: two to three hours a week
2. **Participating in meetings/training**: one hour a quarter or as requested

RESPONSIBILITIES/DUTIES

1. Arrive prior to worship services to double-check and set up equipment as needed.
2. Operate sound recording equipment to record messages and special music for the tape ministry.
3. Label each master audiocassette appropriately with content, and date and keep an organized library of masters.
4. Duplicate audiocassettes as needed.
5. Maintain equipment and arrange for repairs as necessary. Report equipment and supply replacement needs or recommendations to the pastor and/or appropriate committee.

LIGHTING TECHNICIAN

The lighting technician will operate and maintain appropriate lighting in the sanctuary/auditorium during worship services and special events.

Ministry Area/Department	Media
Position	Lighting technician
Accountable To	Executive pastor
Ministry Target	Congregation
Position Is	Volunteer
Position May Be Filled By	Church member
Minimum Maturity Level	New, growing Christian
Spiritual Gifts	Serving
Talents or Abilities Desired	Knowledge of appropriate lighting techniques and ability to adjust lighting as needed • Able to follow cues • Good eyesight
Best Personality Traits	Dependable • Consistent • Leader-analyst or dependable-analyst
Passion For	Creating moods and atmosphere through lighting that is conducive to the worship experience
Length of Service Commitment	One year minimum

ANTICIPATED TIME COMMITMENTS
1. **Doing ministry/preparing for ministry**: three to four hours a week (more during special events)
2. **Participating in meetings/training**: one hour a quarter or as requested

RESPONSIBILITIES/DUTIES
1. Arrive prior to worship services to double-check and set lighting as needed.
2. Operate lights/spotlights as needed during worship services and special events.
3. Report equipment repair and supply needs to building and grounds director or appropriate person.
4. Coordinate lighting needs with the worship director or drama director for worship services and special productions.

PHOTOGRAPHER

The photographer will take photographs for church publications and historical archives and of all new members to display on the bulletin board.

Ministry Area/Department	Media
Position	Photographer
Accountable To	Executive pastor
Ministry Target	Church ministries in general
Position Is	Volunteer
Position May Be Filled By	Church member
Minimum Maturity Level	New, growing Christian
Spiritual Gifts	Serving • Exhortation
Talents or Abilities Desired	Photography experience • Good eyesight • Detail oriented • Own equipment
Best Personality Traits	Pleasant • Professional • Analyst-leader or leader-expresser
Passion For	Capturing special moments • Creating photo memories
Length of Service Commitment	One year minimum

ANTICIPATED TIME COMMITMENTS

1. **Doing ministry/preparing for ministry**: two hours a month—more during special events
2. **Participating in meetings/training**: minimal, as needed

RESPONSIBILITIES/DUTIES

1. Take snapshots of new members for bulletin board.
2. Take photos for churchwide publications.
3. Take photos at special church events.
4. Provide copies of the photos to the historian.

PUBLIC RELATIONS ASSISTANT

The public relations assistant will contribute to good public relations of the church by organizing volunteers to assemble and prepare pieces for mailing and distributing printed materials as necessary.

Ministry Area/Department	Media
Position	Public relations assistant
Accountable To	Public relations coordinator
Ministry Target	Congregation and the community
Position Is	Volunteer
Position May Be Filled By	Church member
Minimum Maturity Level	New, growing Christian
Spiritual Gifts	Serving
Talents or Abilities Desired	Good driver • Own transportation • Enjoys running errands
Best Personality Traits	Team spirit • Servant's heart • Dependable-leader or dependable-expresser
Passion For	Promoting good communication within the church and presenting a positive image of the church to the community
Length of Service Commitment	One year minimum

ANTICIPATED TIME COMMITMENTS

1. **Doing ministry/preparing for ministry**: one hour a week—more during special events
2. **Participating in meetings/training**: one hour a month

RESPONSIBILITIES/DUTIES

1. Assist with delivering or distributing advertisements, flyers and other public relations pieces for the church.
2. Collate, fold, stamp and otherwise prepare special pieces for mailing.

PUBLIC RELATIONS COORDINATOR

The public relations coordinator will oversee church publications and advertising and will offer suggestions for improving and maintaining the church's image in the community.

Ministry Area/Department	Media
Position	Public relations coordinator
Accountable To	Executive pastor
Ministry Target	Congregation and the community
Position Is	Volunteer
Position May Be Filled By	Church member
Minimum Maturity Level	New, growing Christian
Spiritual Gifts	Administration
Talents or Abilities Desired	Experience in publishing, advertising or public relations • Organized • Good communicator
Best Personality Traits	Organizer • Friendly • Professional • Dependable-leader
Passion For	Promoting good communication within the church and presenting a positive image of the church in the community
Length of Service Commitment	One year minimum

ANTICIPATED TIME COMMITMENTS

1. **Doing ministry/preparing for ministry:** one hour a week (more during special events)
2. **Participating in meetings/training:** one hour a month

RESPONSIBILITIES/DUTIES

1. Coordinate and oversee development of advertisements, flyers, public relations pieces, news releases and newsletters for the church.
2. Meet with public relations assistants to brainstorm and delegate tasks and special projects.
3. Contact photographer regarding photography needs.
4. Coordinate and insure completion and delivery of special mailings, neighborhood canvasses, etc.
5. Keep a file of all the church's printed advertisements, newsletters, etc.

PUBLIC RELATIONS GRAPHIC DESIGNER

The public relations graphic designer will contribute to good public relations of the church by using graphic design skills to help develop printed media.

Ministry Area/Department	Media
Position	Public relations graphic designer
Accountable To	Public relations coordinator
Ministry Target	Congregation and the community
Position Is	Volunteer
Position May Be Filled By	Church member
Minimum Maturity Level	New, growing Christian
Spiritual Gifts	Serving
Talents or Abilities Desired	Experience in graphic design • Proficient computer skills
Best Personality Traits	Artistic • Creative • Leader-analyst or leader-dependable
Passion For	Promoting good communication within the church and presenting a positive image of the church to the community
Length of Service Commitment	One year minimum

ANTICIPATED TIME COMMITMENTS

1. **Doing ministry/preparing for ministry:** two hours a week—more during special events
2. **Participating in meetings/training:** one hour a month

RESPONSIBILITIES/DUTIES

1. Work with public relations coordinator and public relations assistants to design advertisements, flyers, public relations pieces, news releases and newsletters for the church.
2. Meet with public relations coordinator and assistants to brainstorm regarding special projects.
3. Use computer skills to create and finalize design and layout of advertisements, flyers, public relations pieces, news releases and newsletters as assigned by the public relations coordinator.

PUBLIC RELATIONS WRITER

The public relations writer will contribute to good public relations by using writing and editing skills to help develop printed media.

Ministry Area/Department	Media
Position	Public relations writer
Accountable To	Public relations coordinator
Ministry Target	Congregation and the community
Position Is	Volunteer
Position May Be Filled By	Church member
Minimum Maturity Level	New, growing Christian
Spiritual Gifts	Serving • Administration
Talents or Abilities Desired	Experience in copywriting and editing • Good communicator
Best Personality Traits	Team spirit • Creative • Analyst-dependable or analyst-expresser
Passion For	Promoting good communication within the church and presenting a positive image of the church in the community
Length of Service Commitment	One year minimum

ANTICIPATED TIME COMMITMENTS

1. **Doing ministry/preparing for ministry:** two hours a week—more during special events
2. **Participating in meetings/training:** one hour a month

RESPONSIBILITIES/DUTIES

1. Work with public relations coordinator and other public relations assistants to develop advertisements, flyers, public relations pieces, news releases and newsletters for the church.
2. Meet with public relations coordinator and assistants to brainstorm regarding special projects.
3. Write articles for the church newsletter. Collect announcements and calendar information, interview ministry sponsors regarding upcoming activities and events, cover special churchwide events, interview church members in each newsletter.
4. Write ad copy.
5. Proofread material to be printed.

Sound Technician

The sound technician will adjust and maintain the sound system to ensure a clear and comfortable sound level within the church facilities.

Ministry Area/Department	Media
Position	Sound technician
Accountable To	Executive pastor
Ministry Target	Congregation
Position Is	Volunteer
Position May Be Filled By	Church member
Minimum Maturity Level	New, growing Christian
Spiritual Gifts	Serving
Talents or Abilities Desired	Familiar with P.A. systems • Experience in operating sound equipment • Good hearing
Best Personality Traits	Consistent • Dependable-analyst
Passion For	Making sure God's message in word and song is heard clearly
Length of Service Commitment	Two years minimum

Anticipated Time Commitments

1. **Doing ministry/preparing for ministry:** two to three hours a week
2. **Participating in meetings/training:** one hour a quarter or as requested

Responsibilities/Duties

1. Arrive prior to worship services to double-check and set up equipment as needed: microphones, monitors, etc.
2. Operate sound equipment during all services and special events held in the church sanctuary/auditorium.
3. Maintain equipment and arrange for repairs as necessary. Report equipment replacement needs or recommendations to the executive pastor and/or appropriate committee.

TAPE MINISTRY DIRECTOR

The tape ministry director will handle all orders for audiocassette or videotape messages and perform special services, from receiving the order/funds to delivering the tapes.

Ministry Area/Department	Media
Position	Tape ministry director
Accountable To	Executive pastor
Ministry Target	Congregation, homebound members and the community
Position Is	Volunteer
Position May Be Filled By	Church member
Minimum Maturity Level	New, growing Christian
Spiritual Gifts	Serving • Administration • Exhortation
Talents or Abilities Desired	Organizational skills
Best Personality Traits	Persistent • Dependable
Passion For	Inspiring and encouraging people through providing messages and music on tape
Length of Service Commitment	One year minimum

ANTICIPATED TIME COMMITMENTS

1. **Doing ministry/preparing for ministry:** one hour a week
2. **Participating in meetings/training:** one hour a quarter or as requested

RESPONSIBILITIES/DUTIES

1. Receive orders for audiocassettes or videotape messages and special services at the church.
2. Give funds received for tapes to the financial secretary.
3. Order tapes from the audio or video technician.
4. Deliver the tapes to the appropriate people either at church, by mail or through outreach ministers.
5. Oversee budget and expenditures for the tape ministry.

VIDEO TECHNICIAN

The video technician will record messages, special services and events; keep an organized library of tape recordings; and provide duplicate videos for the tape ministry.

Ministry Area/Department	Media
Position	Video technician
Accountable To	Executive pastor
Ministry Target	Congregation and the community
Position Is	Volunteer
Position May Be Filled By	Church member
Minimum Maturity Level	New, growing Christian
Spiritual Gifts	Serving
Talents or Abilities Desired	Experience in operating video recording equipment • Good hearing and eyesight
Best Personality Traits	Consistent • Dependable
Passion For	Producing professional quality videos to share God's message with others
Length of Service Commitment	One year minimum

ANTICIPATED TIME COMMITMENTS

1. **Doing ministry/preparing for ministry:** two hours a month (more depending on special events)
2. **Participating in meetings/training:** one hour a quarter or as requested

RESPONSIBILITIES/DUTIES

1. Arrive prior to special service or event, double-check and set up equipment as needed.
2. Operate video camera to videotape special services and events.
3. Edit master videotapes if necessary.
4. Label each master video appropriately with content and date, and keep an organized library of masters.
5. Duplicate videos as needed for the tape ministry.
6. Maintain equipment and arrange for repairs as necessary. Report equipment replacement needs or recommendations to the executive pastor and/or appropriate committee.

MEN'S

MEN'S MINISTRY DIRECTOR

The men's ministry director will organize and lead a ministry that builds up and helps the men of the church become spiritual leaders and provides an avenue of outreach to men in the community.

Ministry Area/Department	Men
Position	Men's ministry director
Accountable To	Associate pastor
Ministry Target	Men in the congregation and community
Position Is	Volunteer
Position May Be Filled By	Church member
Minimum Maturity Level	Stable, maturing Christian
Spiritual Gifts	Administration • Pastor/shepherd • Exhortation
Talents or Abilities Desired	Organizer
Best Personality Traits	Leader • Dependable • Consistent • Good character • Expresser-leader
Passion For	Developing and encouraging men of God
Length of Service Commitment	One year minimum

ANTICIPATED TIME COMMITMENTS

1. **Doing ministry/preparing for ministry**: two to three hours a week
2. **Participating in meetings/training**: one hour a quarter

RESPONSIBILITIES/DUTIES

1. Regularly pray for:
   a. Men in the church;
   b. Families in the church whose men do not attend;
   c. Men in the community at large.
2. Organize and oversee the men's ministry.
   a. Plan special courses for training men to become spiritual leaders in the home, church and community.
   b. Plan at least one yearly retreat for prayer, fellowship and encouragement: a men's rally event, special camp, lake retreat, etc.
   c. Organize small groups that meet regularly for accountability, building relationships and spiritual encouragement through prayer, devotions and sharing. Rearrange into new small groups at regular intervals—perhaps quarterly.
   d. Plan activities and special projects for men only: prayer breakfasts, church improvement day, fishing expedition, father/son event, softball league, etc.

e. Develop a mentoring network where spiritually mature men (or men who have faced specific situations) can identify with and give guidance/support to men going through similar situations.

f. Report special needs to the associate pastor.

g. Oversee budget and expenditures for the men's ministry.

MEN'S SMALL GROUP LEADER

The men's small group leader will organize and lead a small group the purpose of which is to provide accountability, biblical direction and encouragement. The small groups may include men of the church as well as unchurched men who need Christian influence and want to associate with the group.

Ministry Area/Department	Men
Position	Men's small group leader
Accountable To	Men's ministry director
Ministry Target	Men in the congregation and community
Position Is	Volunteer
Position May Be Filled By	Church member
Minimum Maturity Level	Stable, maturing Christian
Spiritual Gifts	Administration • Pastor/shepherd • Exhortation • Teaching • Evangelism
Talents or Abilities Desired	Organizational skills
Best Personality Traits	Leader • Dependable-expresser or dependable-leader • Consistent • Good moral character
Passion For	Developing and encouraging men of God
Length of Service Commitment	One year minimum

ANTICIPATED TIME COMMITMENTS

1. **Doing ministry/preparing for ministry:** two to three hours a week
2. **Participating in meetings/training:** one hour a quarter

RESPONSIBILITIES/DUTIES

1. Regularly pray for the men in your small group.
2. Lead your small group.
   a. Plan brief devotional message or topical Bible study for presentation and discussion at weekly meetings.
   b. Lead in prayer and encourage group participation in prayer.
   c. Lead group to share concerns, answers to prayer, struggles, biblical advice and how others have effectively handled temptations and situations.
   d. Plan one special activity for the group, probably quarterly. This could be a meal together at a restaurant, a trip to a ball game, a fishing trip, picnic or a game of horseshoes at the last group meeting.
   e. Report special needs to the men's ministry director.

MUSIC

CHILDREN'S CHOIR MEMBER

The children's choir member will participate in rehearsals and performances as scheduled.

Ministry Area/Department	Music
Position	Children's choir member
Accountable To	Children's music director
Ministry Target	Children • Congregation • Community
Position Is	Volunteer
Position May Be Filled By	Church member
Minimum Maturity Level	New, growing Christian
Spiritual Gifts	Exhortation • Serving
Talents or Abilities Desired	Love of singing
Best Personality Traits	Friendly • Willing • Dependable-expresser or expresser-analyst
Passion For	Making a joyful noise unto the Lord
Length of Service Commitment	One year minimum

ANTICIPATED TIME COMMITMENTS

1. **Doing ministry/preparing for ministry**: one hour a week; more during special productions
2. **Participating in meetings/training**: one hour a week

RESPONSIBILITIES/DUTIES

1. Participate in rehearsals.
2. Follow directions of the children's music director and assistant.
3. Sing in the children's choir during services and events as scheduled.
4. Practice singing at home; learn songs.

CHILDREN'S MUSIC ASSISTANT

The children's music assistant will assist the children's music director with recruitment, registration, crowd control and as otherwise needed during choir rehearsal and performances.

Ministry Area/Department	Music
Position	Children's music assistant
Accountable To	Children's music director
Ministry Target	Children
Position Is	Volunteer
Position May Be Filled By	Church member
Minimum Maturity Level	New, growing Christian
Spiritual Gifts	Administration • Pastor/shepherd • Exhortation • Serving
Talents or Abilities Desired	Organized • Patient • Loves children
Best Personality Traits	Dependable • Consistent • Good character • Neat • Analyst-expresser or expresser-leader
Passion For	Serving and assisting the children's music director; leading children and instilling in them the value of music
Length of Service Commitment	One year minimum

ANTICIPATED TIME COMMITMENTS

1. **Doing ministry/preparing for ministry:** two to three hours a week; more during special events
2. **Participating in meetings/training:** as needed

RESPONSIBILITIES/DUTIES

1. Work with music director to learn music.
2. Assist with crowd control, discipline and as otherwise needed during weekly children's choir rehearsals.
3. Recruit new members for the children's choir.
4. Register choir members and keep record of name, age, address, phone and parents' names of each.
5. Help direct the children's choir during services and events as scheduled.
6. Encourage and pray for the children's choir members.

CHILDREN'S MUSIC DIRECTOR

The children's music director will organize and direct the children's choir.

Ministry Area/Department	Music
Position	Children's music director
Accountable To	Music director
Ministry Target	Children in the congregation and community
Position Is	Volunteer
Position May Be Filled By	Church member
Minimum Maturity Level	New, growing Christian
Spiritual Gifts	Administration • Exhortation • Pastor/shepherd
Talents or Abilities Desired	Good leadership skills • Organized • Knowledge of music fundamentals • Loves children
Best Personality Traits	Patient • Dependable • Consistent • Neat • Good character
Passion For	Teaching children to praise the Lord through music
Length of Service Commitment	One year minimum

ANTICIPATED TIME COMMITMENTS

1. **Doing ministry/preparing for ministry:** two to three hours a week; more during special events
2. **Participating in meetings/training:** as needed

RESPONSIBILITIES/DUTIES

1. Work in conjunction with music director to select and obtain children's music.
2. Schedule and direct weekly children's choir rehearsals.
3. Recruit new members for the children's choir.
4. Direct the children's choir during services and events as scheduled.
5. Encourage and pray for the children's choir members.
6. Lead music during children's church.
7. Keep parents informed of rehearsals and performances via phone calls, printed announcements, etc.
8. Coordinate with music director and schedule performances—a minimum of three per year.
9. Oversee budget and expenditures for the children's music ministry.

HANDBELL CHOIR DIRECTOR

The handbell choir director will organize and lead the church handbell group in rehearsals and special performances.

Ministry Area/Department	Music
Position	Handbell choir director
Accountable To	Music director
Ministry Target	Congregation
Position Is	Volunteer
Position May Be Filled By	Other approved individual
Minimum Maturity Level	Stable, maturing Christian
Spiritual Gifts	Administration • Exhortation • Pastor/shepherd
Talents or Abilities Desired	Good leadership skills • Organized • Knowledge of handbell and music fundamentals • Experience in directing an instrumental group
Best Personality Traits	Dependable • Consistent • Neat • Good character • Organized
Passion For	Exalting God, exhorting the saints and influencing the lost through music
Length of Service Commitment	One year minimum

ANTICIPATED TIME COMMITMENTS

1. Doing ministry/preparing for ministry: one hour a week; more during special events
2. Participating in meetings/training: as needed

RESPONSIBILITIES/DUTIES

1. Work in conjunction with music director to select and obtain handbell music.
2. Schedule and direct weekly handbell rehearsals.
3. Recruit new members for the handbell group.
4. Direct the handbell performances as scheduled (at least two performances per year).
5. Coordinate schedule for handbell performances with music director.
6. Oversee budget and expenditures for the handbell ministry.

HANDBELL CHOIR MEMBER

The handbell choir member will rehearse and perform with the handbell group when scheduled.

Ministry Area/Department	Music
Position	Handbell choir member
Accountable To	Handbell choir director
Ministry Target	Congregation
Position Is	Volunteer
Position May Be Filled By	Other approved individual
Minimum Maturity Level	New, growing Christian
Spiritual Gifts	Serving • Exhortation
Talents or Abilities Desired	Able to read music and count rhythms
Best Personality Traits	Dependable • Neat • Good character
Passion For	Exalting God, exhorting the saints and influencing the lost through music
Length of Service Commitment	One year minimum

ANTICIPATED TIME COMMITMENTS

1. **Doing ministry/preparing for ministry:** one hour a week (more during special events)
2. **Participating in meetings/training:** as requested

RESPONSIBILITIES/DUTIES

1. Participate in rehearsals.
2. Learn to read music and count rhythms.
3. Perform with the handbell choir when scheduled.

MUSIC DIRECTOR

The music director will organize and lead the music ministry of the church and assist the pastor during worship services.

Ministry Area/Department	Music
Position	Music director
Accountable To	Pastor
Ministry Target	Congregation
Position Is	Paid staff
Position May Be Filled By	Church member
Minimum Maturity Level	Stable, maturing Christian
Spiritual Gifts	Administration • Exhortation • Pastor/shepherd
Talents or Abilities Desired	Good leadership skills • Organizer • Experience in directing a choir or musical group
Best Personality Traits	Dependable • Consistent • Neat • Good character • Organized
Passion For	Exalting God, exhorting the saints and influencing the lost through music
Length of Service Commitment	Two years minimum

ANTICIPATED TIME COMMITMENTS

1. **Doing ministry/preparing for ministry**: eight hours a week; more during special events
2. **Participating in meetings/training**: one hour a week

RESPONSIBILITIES/DUTIES

1. Oversee the entire music ministry of the church.
2. Choose music for and direct the adult choir.
3. Organize, maintain and update the music library.
4. Schedule and direct weekly and special rehearsals.
5. Select music and direct special groups and solos.
6. Provide training for choirs and musical groups.
7. Recruit new members for the music ministry.
8. Select and coordinate congregational songs with sermon topics and seasonal themes. Lead congregational singing.
9. Arrange for special music during every regular service—either by adult choir, special musical groups, soloists, youth or children's choirs.
10. Maintain musical instruments and arrange for tuning and upkeep.
11. Organize and maintain choir robes.

12. Supervise church pianist, organist, orchestra director and youth and children's choir directors.

13. Plan and direct Christmas and Easter musicals.

14. Coordinate with sound technician as needed.

15. Oversee budget and expenditures for the drama ministry.

MUSIC MINISTRY LIBRARIAN

The music ministry librarian will assist the music director in organizing and maintaining the church's library of music.

Ministry Area/Department	Music
Position	Music ministry librarian
Accountable To	Music director
Ministry Target	Church musicians and choirs
Position Is	Volunteer
Position May Be Filled By	Church member
Minimum Maturity Level	New, growing Christian
Spiritual Gifts	Administration • Serving
Talents or Abilities Desired	Good organizational skills
Best Personality Traits	Dependable • Neat • Organized
Passion For	Keeping music library in order for music ministry
Length of Service Commitment	One year minimum

ANTICIPATED TIME COMMITMENTS

1. **Doing ministry/preparing for ministry:** one hour a week
2. **Participating in meetings/training:** as requested

RESPONSIBILITIES/DUTIES

1. Work in conjunction with music director to organize storage of sheet music, music books and accompaniment music on tape or CD.
2. Catalog/keep inventory of all music in the library.
3. File or locate music as needed.
4. Repair torn music sheets/books.

ORCHESTRA DIRECTOR

The orchestra director will organize and lead the church orchestra for performances in regular Sunday services and occasional special events.

Ministry Area/Department	Music
Position	Orchestra director
Accountable To	Music director
Ministry Target	Congregation
Position Is	Volunteer
Position May Be Filled By	Other approved individual
Minimum Maturity Level	Stable, maturing Christian
Spiritual Gifts	Administration • Pastor/shepherd • Exhortation
Talents or Abilities Desired	Good leadership and organizational skills • Training and/or experience in directing an orchestra or instrumental group
Best Personality Traits	Dependable • Consistent • Good character • Neat • Organized
Passion For	Exalting God, exhorting the saints and influencing the lost through music
Length of Service Commitment	One year minimum

ANTICIPATED TIME COMMITMENTS

1. **Doing ministry/preparing for ministry**: three hours a week (more during special events)
2. **Participating in meetings/training**: thirty minutes a week

RESPONSIBILITIES/DUTIES

1. Work in conjunction with music director to obtain orchestra music.
2. Schedule and direct weekly orchestra rehearsals.
3. Select orchestra music for special events.
4. Recruit new members for the orchestra.
5. Direct the orchestra during Sunday morning services and special events.
6. Oversee budget and expenditures for the orchestra ministry.

ORCHESTRA MEMBER

The orchestra member will play with the church orchestra during performances in regular Sunday services and occasional special events.

Ministry Area/Department	Music
Position	Orchestra member
Accountable To	Orchestra director
Ministry Target	Congregation
Position Is	Volunteer
Position May Be Filled By	Other approved individual
Minimum Maturity Level	New, growing Christian
Spiritual Gifts	Exhortation • Serving
Talents or Abilities Desired	Musical talent and skill in playing an instrument used in an orchestra
Best Personality Traits	Dependable • Consistent
Passion For	Exalting God, exhorting the saints and influencing the lost through music
Length of Service Commitment	One year minimum

ANTICIPATED TIME COMMITMENTS

1. **Doing ministry/preparing for ministry:** two to three hours a week, more during special events
2. **Participating in meetings/training:** as requested

RESPONSIBILITIES/DUTIES

1. Participate in weekly orchestra rehearsals.
2. Be able to read/play music on at least a high school level.
3. Practice music on own time.
4. Perform with the orchestra during Sunday morning services and special events: seasonal celebrations, dramas or musicals
5. May need to provide own instrument.

ORGANIST

The organist will play the organ for the choir during rehearsals when requested and for the choir and congregation during church services.

Ministry Area/Department	Music
Position	Organist
Accountable To	Music director
Ministry Target	Choirs and congregation
Position Is	Volunteer/paid staff
Position May Be Filled By	Other approved individual
Minimum Maturity Level	New, growing Christian
Spiritual Gifts	Exhortation • Serving
Talents or Abilities Desired	Experience and ability to play hymns and special music on the organ
Best Personality Traits	Dependable • Consistent • Good character • Neat • Organized • Supportive
Passion For	Exalting God, exhorting the saints and influencing the lost through music
Length of Service Commitment	One year minimum

ANTICIPATED TIME COMMITMENTS

1. **Doing ministry/preparing for ministry:** four to five hours a week, more during special events
2. **Participating in meetings/training:** one hour a week

RESPONSIBILITIES/DUTIES

1. Play organ during regularly scheduled services.
2. Play as scheduled for special services: revivals, concerts, seasonal programs, etc.
3. Play for choir practice as scheduled.
4. Play during offertories as scheduled.
5. **Optional:** Play during weddings and funerals as employed by the individuals requesting such services.

PIANIST

The pianist will play the piano for the choir during rehearsals and for the choir and congregation during church services.

Ministry Area/Department	Music
Position	Pianist
Accountable To	Music director
Ministry Target	Choirs and congregation
Position Is	Volunteer/paid staff
Position May Be Filled By	Other approved individual
Minimum Maturity Level	New, growing Christian
Spiritual Gifts	Exhortation • Serving
Talents or Abilities Desired	Experience and ability to play hymns and special music on the piano • Good organizational skills • Neat appearance
Best Personality Traits	Dependable-expresser • Consistent • Good character
Passion For	Exalting God, exhorting the saints and influencing the lost through music
Length of Service Commitment	One year minimum

ANTICIPATED TIME COMMITMENTS

1. **Doing ministry/preparing for ministry:** four to five hours a week—more during special events
2. **Participating in meetings/training:** one hour a week

RESPONSIBILITIES/DUTIES

1. Play piano during regularly scheduled services.
2. Play as scheduled for special services: revivals, concerts, seasonal programs, etc.
3. Play for choir practice as scheduled.
4. Play during offertories as scheduled.
5. **Optional:** Play during weddings and funerals as employed by the individuals requesting such services.

PRAISE TEAM LEADER

The praise team leader will organize and lead the church praise team in presenting special praise and worship music to the congregation and leading the congregation in praise and worship.

Ministry Area/Department	Music
Position	Praise team leader
Accountable To	Music director
Ministry Target	Congregation and praise team
Position Is	Volunteer
Position May Be Filled By	Church member
Minimum Maturity Level	Stable, maturing Christian
Spiritual Gifts	Administration • Pastor/shepherd • Exhortation
Talents or Abilities Desired	Good leadership and organizational skills • Training and/or experience in directing a choir or music group preferred • Knowledge of basic music fundamentals
Best Personality Traits	Dependable • Consistent • Good character • Neat • Outgoing • Expresser-leader
Passion For	For praising and worshiping God through music
Length of Service Commitment	One year minimum

ANTICIPATED TIME COMMITMENTS

1. **Doing ministry/preparing for ministry:** two hours a week
2. **Participating in meetings/training:** one hour a week

RESPONSIBILITIES/DUTIES

1. Work in conjunction with music director to obtain praise music.
2. Organize praise team(s).
3. Schedule praise team rehearsals.
4. Recruit members for the praise team(s).
5. Lead the praise team in leading the congregation in praise music and in presenting special music.

PRAISE TEAM MEMBER

The praise team member will present special praise and worship music to the congregation and encourage the congregation to join in praise and worship.

Ministry Area/Department	Music
Position	Praise team member
Accountable To	Praise team leader
Ministry Target	Congregation
Position Is	Volunteer
Position May Be Filled By	Church member
Minimum Maturity Level	New, growing Christian
Spiritual Gifts	Exhortation • Serving
Talents or Abilities Desired	Good singing voice and/or able to play musical instrument
Best Personality Traits	Good character • Neat • Outgoing • Dependable-expresser or expresser-analyst
Passion For	Praising and worshiping God through music
Length of Service Commitment	One year minimum

ANTICIPATED TIME COMMITMENTS

1. **Doing ministry/preparing for ministry:** two hours a week
2. **Participating in meetings/training:** as requested

RESPONSIBILITIES/DUTIES

1. Participate in rehearsals as scheduled.
2. Participate with the praise team in leading the congregation in praise music and in presenting special music.

PRESCHOOL CHOIR MEMBER

The preschool choir member will participate in rehearsals and performances as scheduled.

Ministry Area/Department	Music
Position	Preschool choir member
Accountable To	Preschool music director
Ministry Target	Congregation
Position Is	Volunteer
Position May Be Filled By	Regular attendee
Minimum Maturity Level	New, growing Christian or growing interest in spiritual matters
Spiritual Gifts	Exhortation • Serving
Talents or Abilities Desired	Love of singing
Best Personality Traits	Friendly • Willing
Passion For	Making a joyful noise unto the Lord
Length of Service Commitment	One year minimum

ANTICIPATED TIME COMMITMENTS

1. **Doing ministry/preparing for ministry**: one hour a week—more during special productions
2. **Participating in meetings/training**: does not apply

RESPONSIBILITIES/DUTIES

1. Participate in rehearsals.
2. Follow direction of the preschool music director and assistant.
3. Sing during services and events as scheduled.
4. Practice singing at home; learn songs.

PRESCHOOL MUSIC ASSISTANT

The preschool music assistant will assist the preschool music director with recruitment, registration, crowd control and as otherwise needed during choir rehearsal and performances.

Ministry Area/Department	Music
Position	Preschool music assistant
Accountable To	Preschool music director
Ministry Target	Preschoolers and preschool music director
Position Is	Volunteer
Position May Be Filled By	Church member
Minimum Maturity Level	New, growing Christian
Spiritual Gifts	Administration • Pastor/shepherd • Exhortation • Serving
Talents or Abilities Desired	Good organizational skills • Patient • Love children
Best Personality Traits	Consistent • Good character • Neat • Expresser-leader or dependable-expresser
Passion For	Serving and assisting the preschool music director • Leading children and instilling in them the value of music in praising God
Length of Service Commitment	One year minimum

ANTICIPATED TIME COMMITMENTS

1. **Doing ministry/preparing for ministry:** two to three hours a week—more during special events
2. **Participating in meetings/training:** fifteen minutes a week

RESPONSIBILITIES/DUTIES

1. Work with music director to learn music.
2. Assist with crowd control, discipline and as otherwise needed during preschool choir rehearsals.
3. Recruit new members for the preschool choir.
4. Register choir members and keep record of name, age, address, phone and parents' names of each.
5. Help direct the preschool choir during services and events as scheduled.
6. Encourage and pray for the preschool choir members.

PRESCHOOL MUSIC DIRECTOR

The preschool music director will organize and direct the preschool choir.

Ministry Area/Department	Music
Position	Preschool music director
Accountable To	Music director
Ministry Target	Preschool children • Congregation
Position Is	Volunteer
Position May Be Filled By	Church member
Minimum Maturity Level	New, growing Christian
Spiritual Gifts	Administration • Pastor/shepherd • Exhortation
Talents or Abilities Desired	Good leadership and organizational skills • Knowledge of music fundamentals • Patience • Love children
Best Personality Traits	Consistent • Good character • Neat • Expresser-leader or expresser-dependable
Passion For	Teaching children to serve the Lord through music
Length of Service Commitment	One year minimum

ANTICIPATED TIME COMMITMENTS

1. **Doing ministry/preparing for ministry:** two to three hours a week
2. **Participating in meetings/training:** fifteen minutes a week

RESPONSIBILITIES/DUTIES

1. Work with music director to select and obtain preschool children's music.
2. Schedule and direct weekly preschool choir rehearsals.
3. Recruit new members for the preschool choir.
4. Direct the preschool choir during services and events as scheduled.
5. Encourage and pray for the preschool choir members.
6. Keep parents informed of rehearsals and performances: phone calls and printed announcements.
7. Schedule performances with music director—minimum three per year.
8. Oversee budget and expenditures for the preschool music ministry.

SANCTUARY CHOIR MEMBER

The sanctuary choir member will present special music as part of every Sunday's worship experience and will participate in special musicals as planned.

Ministry Area/Department	Music
Position	Sanctuary choir member
Accountable To	Music director
Ministry Target	Congregation
Position Is	Volunteer
Position May Be Filled By	Church member
Minimum Maturity Level	New, growing Christian
Spiritual Gifts	Exhortation • Serving
Talents or Abilities Desired	Able to sing in key • Enjoy singing
Best Personality Traits	Good character • Neat • Expresser-dependable or expresser-analyst
Passion For	Praising and worshiping God • Influencing the lost • Encouraging the saints through music
Length of Service Commitment	One year minimum

ANTICIPATED TIME COMMITMENTS

1. **Doing ministry/preparing for ministry:** two to three hours a week
2. **Participating in meetings/training:** as requested

RESPONSIBILITIES/DUTIES

1. Participate in rehearsals as scheduled.
2. Perform with the choir on Sunday mornings and other times as scheduled.
3. Be available for additional rehearsals and performances for special seasonal musicals at least once a year.

YOUTH CHOIR ASSISTANT

The youth choir assistant will assist the youth music director with recruitment, registration, crowd control and as otherwise needed during choir rehearsal and performances.

Ministry Area/Department	Music
Position	Youth music assistant
Accountable To	Youth music director
Ministry Target	Youth and youth choir director
Position Is	Volunteer
Position May Be Filled By	Church member
Minimum Maturity Level	New, growing Christian
Spiritual Gifts	Administration • Pastor/shepherd • Exhortation • Serving
Talents or Abilities Desired	Good organizational skills • Love and patience for teens • Understanding of the challenges of adolescents • Valid driver's license
Best Personality Traits	Consistent • Good character • Neat • Expresser-dependable or expresser-analyst
Passion For	Serving and assisting the youth music director • Leading youth and instilling in them the value of music in praising God and reaching others
Length of Service Commitment	One year minimum

ANTICIPATED TIME COMMITMENTS

1. **Doing ministry/preparing for ministry:** one to two hours a week (more during special events)
2. **Participating in meetings/training:** thirty minutes a week

RESPONSIBILITIES/DUTIES

1. Work with youth choir director to learn music.
2. Assist with crowd control, discipline and as otherwise needed during youth choir rehearsals.
3. Recruit new members for the youth choir.
4. Register choir members and keep records of name, age, address, phone and parents' names of each.
5. Help direct the youth choir during services and events as scheduled.
6. Encourage and pray for the youth choir members.
7. Assist with transportation to special performances, if needed.

YOUTH CHOIR DIRECTOR

The youth choir director will organize and direct the youth choir.

Ministry Area/Department	Music
Position	Youth choir director
Accountable To	Music director
Ministry Target	Youth, congregation and community
Position Is	Volunteer
Position May Be Filled By	Church member
Minimum Maturity Level	Stable, maturing Christian
Spiritual Gifts	Administration • Pastor/shepherd • Exhortation
Talents or Abilities Desired	Good leadership and organizational skills • Knowledge of music fundamentals • Love and patience for teens
Best Personality Traits	Dependable • Consistent • Good character • Neat • Expresser-leader
Passion For	Teaching teens to serve the Lord through music
Length of Service Commitment	One year minimum

ANTICIPATED TIME COMMITMENTS

1. **Doing ministry/preparing for ministry**: one to two hours a week
2. **Participating in meetings/training**: thirty minutes a week

RESPONSIBILITIES/DUTIES

1. Work in conjunction with music director to select and obtain youth music.
2. Schedule and direct weekly youth choir rehearsals.
3. Recruit new members for the youth choir.
4. Direct the youth choir during services and special performances as scheduled.
5. Encourage and pray for the youth choir members.
6. Keep parents informed of rehearsals and performances: phone calls, printed announcements.
7. Schedule performances with music director—minimum three per year.
8. Schedule special performances in the community: nursing homes, other churches, school variety shows, etc.
9. Oversee budget and expenditures for the youth choir ministry.

YOUTH CHOIR MEMBER

The youth choir member will participate in rehearsals and performances as scheduled.

Ministry Area/Department	Music
Position	Youth choir member
Accountable To	Youth choir director
Ministry Target	Congregation and community
Position Is	Volunteer
Position May Be Filled By	Regular attendee
Minimum Maturity Level	New, growing Christian or growing interest in spiritual matters
Spiritual Gifts	Exhortation • Serving
Talents or Abilities Desired	Love of singing
Best Personality Traits	Friendly • Willing • Good character • Expresser-analyst or expresser-dependable
Passion For	Making a joyful noise unto the Lord • Influencing the church and community for Christ
Length of Service Commitment	One year minimum

ANTICIPATED TIME COMMITMENTS

1. **Doing ministry/preparing for ministry:** one to two hours a week (more during special productions)
2. **Participating in meetings/training:** as requested

RESPONSIBILITIES/DUTIES

1. Participate in rehearsals.
2. Follow direction of the youth music director and assistant.
3. Sing in the youth choir during church services and special performances in the community.
4. Practice singing at home; learn songs.

YOUTH PRAISE BAND DIRECTOR

The youth praise band director will organize and lead the youth praise band for performances in youth meetings and other services as scheduled.

Ministry Area/Department	Music
Position	Youth praise band leader
Accountable To	Music director
Ministry Target	Congregation and youth
Position Is	Volunteer
Position May Be Filled By	Church member
Minimum Maturity Level	New, growing Christian
Spiritual Gifts	Administration • Pastor/shepherd • Exhortation
Talents or Abilities Desired	Leadership and organizational skills • Ability or experience in directing a music group/band • Knowledge of instruments and skill in playing at least one instrument in the band
Best Personality Traits	Dependable • Consistent • Good character • Neat • Organized
Passion For	Exalting God, exhorting the saints and influencing the lost through music
Length of Service Commitment	One year minimum

ANTICIPATED TIME COMMITMENTS

1. **Doing ministry/preparing for ministry:** one to two hours a week—more during special events
2. **Participating in meetings/training:** one hour a week

RESPONSIBILITIES/DUTIES

1. Work in conjunction with music director to obtain music.
2. Schedule and direct rehearsals.
3. Recruit new members for the praise band.
4. Direct the praise band during youth meetings and other services when scheduled.
5. Coordinate with music director a schedule for playing during church services.
6. Oversee budget and expenditures for the youth praise band ministry.

YOUTH PRAISE BAND MEMBER

The youth praise band member will play with the youth praise band during performances in weekly youth meetings and as scheduled for other services and special events.

Ministry Area/Department	Music
Position	Youth praise band member
Accountable To	Youth praise band director
Ministry Target	Congregation • Youth
Position Is	Volunteer
Position May Be Filled By	Church member
Minimum Maturity Level	New, growing Christian
Spiritual Gifts	Exhortation • Serving
Talents or Abilities Desired	Musical talent • Skill in playing a band instrument
Best Personality Traits	Dependable • Good character • Neat
Passion For	Exalting God, exhorting the saints and influencing the lost through music
Length of Service Commitment	One year minimum

ANTICIPATED TIME COMMITMENTS

1. **Doing ministry/preparing for ministry:** one to two hours a week—more during special events
2. **Participating in meetings/training:** as requested

RESPONSIBILITIES/DUTIES

1. Participate in weekly praise band rehearsals.
2. Be able to read/play music on at least a high school level.
3. Practice music on your own time.
4. Perform with the praise band during weekly youth meetings and when scheduled for other church services or events.
5. Provide own instrument when necessary.

NURSERY

NURSERY CAREGIVER

The nursery caregiver will provide proper care and nurturing to babies/toddlers during church services and special events.

Ministry Area/Department	Nursery
Position	Nursery caregiver
Accountable To	Nursery coordinator
Ministry Target	Babies and their parents
Position Is	Volunteer
Position May Be Filled By	Other approved individual
Minimum Maturity Level	New, growing Christian
Spiritual Gifts	Teaching • Pastor/shepherd • Mercy-showing • Serving
Talents or Abilities Desired	Loves and is able to care for babies and toddlers • No criminal record of child abuse or violent crimes
Best Personality Traits	Loving • Levelheaded • Dependable-expresser
Passion For	Showing God's love to parents and babies through providing loving care and Christian nurturing to babies
Length of Service Commitment	One year minimum

ANTICIPATED TIME COMMITMENTS

1. **Doing ministry/preparing for ministry:** one-and-a-half hours a week
2. **Participating in meetings/training:** quarterly or as requested

RESPONSIBILITIES/DUTIES

1. Arrive at least 15 minutes prior to service or event—earlier if expecting a larger crowd for special services or events.
2. Become familiar with nursery policies and facilities.
3. Greet parents and sign in/out babies/toddlers.
4. Take care of babies/toddlers in the nursery, following nursery policies for safety and proper care:
   a. Change diapers/clothing as necessary; check diapers near end of service.
   b. Rock, play with, sing to, play music for and show picture books to babies/toddlers.
   c. Feed babies when needed or as requested by parents.
   d. Give snacks to toddlers.
5. Change crib sheets after babies/toddlers have been picked up.
6. Place dirty toys in container to be cleaned/disinfected.

NURSERY COORDINATOR

The nursery coordinator will oversee and coordinate the nursery ministry.

Ministry Area/Department	Nursery
Position	Nursery coordinator
Accountable To	Christian education director
Ministry Target	Babies and their parents
Position Is	Volunteer
Position May Be Filled By	Church member
Minimum Maturity Level	New, growing Christian
Spiritual Gifts	Administration • Serving • Pastor/shepherd
Talents or Abilities Desired	Organized • Loves babies and children • No criminal record
Best Personality Traits	Cheerful • Kind • Dependable-leader
Passion For	Protecting, caring for and showing love of Christ to young ones • Offering a safe environment where parents are comfortable leaving their little ones
Length of Service Commitment	One year minimum

ANTICIPATED TIME COMMITMENTS

1. **Doing ministry/preparing for ministry:** two hours a week
2. **Participating in meetings/training:** one hour a quarter

RESPONSIBILITIES/DUTIES

1. Recruit and train volunteers to serve in the nursery.
2. Organize the nursery and ensure its cleanliness and safety.
3. Develop, post and enforce nursery policies.
4. Routinely inspect nursery equipment, toys and supplies:
   a. Report repair and maintenance needs to appropriate personnel.
   b. Restock supplies when needed.
5. Obtain and keep a library of picture books and music/songs on cassettes or CDs for use in the nursery.
6. Keep a current list of nursery caregivers with names/addresses/phone numbers.
7. Schedule nursery caregivers for every service and special churchwide event in which nursery care is needed.
8. Collect and launder used crib sheets weekly.
9. Clean/disinfect dirty toys as necessary.
10. Oversee budget and expenditures for the nursery ministry.

OUTREACH/INREACH

BENEVOLENCE MINISTER

The benevolence minister will serve on a task group to assist church and community members with special needs during crisis situations: unemployed, housing catastrophe, temporarily disabled/hospitalized, unexpected expenses, etc.

Ministry Area/Department	Outreach/Inreach
Position	Benevolence minister
Accountable To	Pastor
Ministry Target	Congregation and community
Position Is	Volunteer
Position May Be Filled By	Church member
Minimum Maturity Level	New, growing Christian
Spiritual Gifts	Mercy-showing • Pastor/shepherd • Serving • Giving
Talents or Abilities Desired	Able to communicate well • Valid driver's license • Own transportation
Best Personality Traits	Compassionate • Expressive • Intuitive • Discerning • Discreet
Passion For	Helping people in need
Length of Service Commitment	Two years minimum

ANTICIPATED TIME COMMITMENTS

1. **Doing ministry/preparing for ministry:** one hour a week
2. **Participating in meetings/training:** as necessary

RESPONSIBILITIES/DUTIES

1. Serve on a task group of benevolence ministers.
2. Work with task group to consider benevolent requests and verify needs.
3. Collect and receive donations of money, nonperishable food items, clothing and other needs for distribution in the benevolence ministry.
4. Contact financial secretary to request funds from budget when needed.
5. Contact those who need benevolence ministry services and arrange to deliver provisions, or schedule a time for them to stop by the church to receive assistance.

BEREAVEMENT MINISTER

The bereavement minister will serve on a task group to offer emotional, spiritual and physical support to church members and regular attendees who are grieving the loss of a loved one.

Ministry Area/Department	Outreach/Inreach
Position	Bereavement minister
Accountable To	Pastor
Ministry Target	Congregation
Position Is	Volunteer
Position May Be Filled By	Church member
Minimum Maturity Level	New, growing Christian
Spiritual Gifts	Mercy-showing • Pastor/shepherd • Serving • Giving • Exhortation
Talents or Abilities Desired	Compassion for grieving people • Good listener • Able to organize groups to assist with special needs during funeral and bereavement period
Best Personality Traits	Compassionate • Dependable-expresser
Passion For	Comforting and helping people who have experienced loss and are grieving
Length of Service Commitment	Two years minimum

ANTICIPATED TIME COMMITMENTS

1. **Doing ministry/preparing for ministry:** varies greatly depending on need; may go a few months with no hours, then several hours in a month.
2. **Participating in meetings/training:** as requested

RESPONSIBILITIES/DUTIES

1. Minister to the bereaved by visiting in the home and by visiting the family at the funeral home.
2. Stay in the home or arrange to have another bereavement minister stay in the home during the funeral to accept deliveries of food, flowers, etc. and to protect empty house during such times.
3. Contact funeral dinner chairperson to arrange meals for the family.
4. Pick up and deliver a cheerful flower arrangement to the home to use as a centerpiece.
5. Offer assistance with errands, transportation and other special needs during week following the loss.
6. Send a thinking-of-you card to the family two weeks after the funeral.

7. Call to touch base with the family three weeks after the funeral.

8. Pray for the family daily for the first month, then as often as they come to mind.

BREAD/COOKIE BAKER

The bread/cookie baker is responsible for providing fresh-baked bread or cookies for delivery to Sunday morning visitors. **Note:** The goal is to have enough people participate in this ministry so that each one only has to provide baked goods once a month.

Ministry Area/Department	Outreach/Inreach
Position	Bread/cookie baker
Accountable To	Bread/cookie visitation coordinator
Ministry Target	Visitors
Position Is	Volunteer
Position May Be Filled By	Church member
Minimum Maturity Level	New, growing Christian
Spiritual Gifts	Serving • Exhortation
Talents or Abilities Desired	Good baking skills
Best Personality Traits	Dependable
Passion For	Baking and extending hospitality
Length of Service Commitment	One year minimum

ANTICIPATED TIME COMMITMENTS

1. **Doing ministry/preparing for ministry:** one hour a week
2. **Participating in meetings/training:** as requested

RESPONSIBILITIES/DUTIES

1. Bake homemade bread and/or cookies to be used in the weekly visitation program.
2. Deliver the fresh-baked goods to the church kitchen on Sunday mornings. You may bake freezable items a week ahead of time and place them in the freezer, but fresh is best!

BREAD/COOKIE TAKER

The bread/cookie taker is responsible for delivering the bread/cookie bag or basket to Sunday morning visitors on Sunday afternoon. **Note:** The goal is to have enough people participate in this ministry so that each one only has to deliver baked goods once a month.

Ministry Area/Department	Outreach/Inreach
Position	Bread/cookie taker
Accountable To	Bread/cookie visitation coordinator
Ministry Target	Visitors
Position Is	Volunteer
Position May Be Filled By	Church member
Minimum Maturity Level	New, growing Christian
Spiritual Gifts	Serving • Exhortation
Talents or Abilities Desired	Valid driver's license • Own transportation • Familiarity with community • Comfortable using maps/following directions
Best Personality Traits	Dependable-expresser • Friendly
Passion For	Making a positive impact on visitors
Length of Service Commitment	One year minimum

ANTICIPATED TIME COMMITMENTS

1. **Doing ministry/preparing for ministry:** one to two hours a week
2. **Participating in meetings/training:** as requested

RESPONSIBILITIES/DUTIES

1. Pick up bags/baskets from coordinator after Sunday morning services and deliver them to visitors—names/addresses to be attached.
2. When you deliver, do not have a lengthy visit. Simply introduce yourself and offer a brief explanation of the visit such as, "Here's a gift from (church name) to let you know we are glad you visited with us today and to invite you to come again."
3. Be familiar with the ministries of the church in case the visitor should ask any questions regarding ministries.

BREAD/COOKIE VISITATION COORDINATOR

The bread/cookie visitation coordinator is responsible for organizing and overseeing the bread/cookie outreach program. **Note:** Internet programs are available that will provide maps showing directions from the church to specific delivery points. Many chambers of commerce also offer city/town maps.

Ministry Area/Department	Outreach/Inreach
Position	Bread/cookie visitation coordinator
Accountable To	Outreach director
Ministry Target	Visitors
Position Is	Volunteer
Position May Be Filled By	Church member
Minimum Maturity Level	New, growing Christian
Spiritual Gifts	Serving • Exhortation • Administration
Talents or Abilities Desired	Strong organizational skills
Best Personality Traits	Dependable-analyst • Expressor-analyst
Passion For	Making a positive impact on visitors
Length of Service Commitment	One year minimum

ANTICIPATED TIME COMMITMENTS

1. **Doing ministry/preparing for ministry:** one to two hours a week
2. **Participating in meetings/training:** as requested

RESPONSIBILITIES/DUTIES

1. Schedule/coordinate/oversee the bakers and takers.
2. Collect visitor information from Sunday School department and ushers at end of Sunday morning services.
3. After collecting information, prepare a bag or basket containing homebaked bread or cookies and a welcome/thank-you note from the church. Attach name/address so that takers will know where to deliver.
4. Make sure the bread/cookie takers pick up the bags or baskets to be delivered Sunday afternoon.

CART WORKER

The Christian Action Repair Team (CART) worker will participate in an ongoing ministry to serve needy members of the church and community by doing construction work and home repairs free of charge.

Ministry Area/Department	Outreach/Inreach
Position	CART worker
Accountable To	Outreach director
Ministry Target	Needy within congregation and community
Position Is	Volunteer
Position May Be Filled By	Church member
Minimum Maturity Level	New, growing Christian
Spiritual Gifts	Serving • Giving
Talents or Abilities Desired	Skilled in housing construction/repair: carpentry, plumbing, electrical, masonry, painting, landscaping, etc.
Best Personality Traits	Dependable-expresser or leader-analyst • Team spirited • Hardworking
Passion For	Using God-given skills to help the needy
Length of Service Commitment	One year minimum

ANTICIPATED TIME COMMITMENTS

1. **Doing ministry/preparing for ministry:** two to eight hours a month, or as many hours as you are able
2. **Participating in meetings/training:** one hour a month

RESPONSIBILITIES/DUTIES

1. Work with other CART workers to do repairs and construction-related work for the needy in the church and community: elderly, disabled, low-income, etc.
2. Obtain materials necessary to do the jobs, either through donations of supplies and money or from church budget as available. In some cases, the person may already have the supplies, but not be able to afford the labor cost.
3. Discuss potential CART jobs and develop a schedule with other CART members.
4. Pray for the people to whom CART ministers and for the resources to continue the ministry.

CHEERLEADER

The cheerleader (male/female) is responsible for offering encouragement and physical assistance to cheer up church members or regular attendees with special needs and circumstances.

Ministry Area/Department	Outreach/Inreach
Position	Cheerleader
Accountable To	Pastor or associate pastor
Ministry Target	Ill or hospitalized church members
Position Is	Volunteer
Position May Be Filled By	Church member
Minimum Maturity Level	New, growing Christian
Spiritual Gifts	Serving • Mercy-showing • Administration
Talents or Abilities Desired	Organizational skills • Gets along well with other people
Best Personality Traits	Dependable-expresser • Compassionate
Passion For	Comforting and encouraging those who are ill
Length of Service Commitment	One year minimum

ANTICIPATED TIME COMMITMENTS

1. **Doing ministry/preparing for ministry:** one to two hours a week
2. **Participating in meetings/training:** as requested

RESPONSIBILITIES/DUTIES

1. Coordinate with other cheerleaders to arrange for meal preparation and delivery to homes of church members or regular attendees who are hospitalized or are at home recuperating from surgery or childbirth, who are ill, etc.
2. Send get-well cards, thinking-of-you cards, sympathy cards or others as appropriate to cheer and encourage fellow church members.
3. Visit hospitalized members and regular attendees.
4. Call those who are sick to find out if they need assistance: transportation to doctor; pick up prescription or groceries; clean house, etc. Run those errands or arrange for someone else to assist when needed.
5. Pray for members and regular attendees who have special needs or are going through trying times.

EVANGELISM ASSISTANT

The evangelism assistant is responsible for assisting the evangelism director with organizing visits, following up leads and participating in the visitation program, including being able to share personal testimony and lead someone to Christ.

Ministry Area/Department	Outreach/Inreach
Position	Evangelism assistant
Accountable To	Evangelism director
Ministry Target	Church visitors and unchurched community members
Position Is	Volunteer
Position May Be Filled By	Church member
Minimum Maturity Level	New, growing Christian
Spiritual Gifts	Administration • Evangelism
Talents or Abilities Desired	Good organizational skills
Best Personality Traits	Expresser-leader or expresser-analyst
Passion For	Leading people to Christ • Helping others in their spiritual growth
Length of Service Commitment	One year minimum

ANTICIPATED TIME COMMITMENTS

1. **Doing ministry/preparing for ministry:** one to two hours a week
2. **Participating in meetings/training:** as requested

RESPONSIBILITIES/DUTIES

1. Follow up with visitors and prospects who have completed forms requesting prayer, asking questions about the ministry, indicating curiosity about salvation, etc.
2. Assist evangelism director with organizing/assigning visits to prospects.
3. Serve as an altar counselor for those who come forward for salvation during or following church services.
4. Pray regularly for the evangelism ministry, for those who will be visited and for specific names of people needing salvation.
5. Be able to share your faith with others, using own life experiences and testimony as well as Scripture.
6. Be familiar with Scriptures that explain how to become a Christian and provide assurance of salvation.

EVANGELISM DIRECTOR

The evangelism director is responsible for overseeing and implementing the church evangelism program, training volunteers and actively participating in the evangelism ministry to influence others for Christ and bring them into the church.

Ministry Area/Department	Outreach/Inreach
Position	Evangelism director
Accountable To	Pastor
Ministry Target	Visitors and unchurched community members
Position Is	Volunteer
Position May Be Filled By	Church member
Minimum Maturity Level	Stable, maturing Christian
Spiritual Gifts	Administration • Evangelism
Talents or Abilities Desired	Good organizational skills
Best Personality Traits	Expresser-leader or analyst-leader
Passion For	Leading people to Christ • Helping others in their spiritual growth
Length of Service Commitment	One year minimum

ANTICIPATED TIME COMMITMENTS

1. **Doing ministry/preparing for ministry:** two hours a week
2. **Participating in meetings/training:** one hour a month

RESPONSIBILITIES/DUTIES

1. Follow up with visitors and prospects who have completed forms requesting prayer, asking questions about the ministry, indicating curiosity about salvation, etc.
2. Work with evangelism assistant to organize and assign visits to prospects.
3. Serve as an altar counselor for those who come forward for salvation during or following church services.
4. Pray regularly for the evangelism ministry, for those who will be visited and for specific names of people needing salvation.
5. Be able to share your faith with others, using own life experiences and testimony as well as Scripture.
6. Be familiar with Scriptures that explain how to become a Christian and provide assurance of salvation.
7. Provide training to those who become involved in the evangelism ministry.
   a. Provide ongoing support and training materials as needed.

    b. Plan a course or seminar at least yearly for training and reinforcement of evangelism methods and church's evangelism program. Teach what to do and what not to do, explore new opportunities, etc.

8. Work with small-group director to plan evangelistic event and follow-up related to small groups.

9. Assist evangelism event coordinator with planning and follow-up.

EVANGELISM EVENT COORDINATOR

The evangelism event coordinator is responsible for including an evangelistic emphasis in church special events and for planning, organizing and overseeing special evangelistic events.

Ministry Area/Department	Outreach/Inreach
Position	Evangelism event coordinator
Accountable To	Evangelism director
Ministry Target	Visitors and unchurched community members
Position Is	Volunteer
Position May Be Filled By	Church member
Minimum Maturity Level	Stable, maturing Christian
Spiritual Gifts	Administration • Evangelism • Exhortation
Talents or Abilities Desired	Organizational skills • Good at pulling people together
Best Personality Traits	Expresser-analyst
Passion For	Leading people to Christ • Helping others in their spiritual growth
Length of Service Commitment	One year minimum

ANTICIPATED TIME COMMITMENTS

1. **Doing ministry/preparing for ministry**: two hours a week
2. **Participating in meetings/training**: one hour a month

RESPONSIBILITIES/DUTIES

1. Plan, organize and oversee at least one major evangelistic event per year: ministry fair, revival, special seminar, Friend Day, etc.
2. Work with other ministry leaders to include an evangelistic emphasis in their special events: seasonal services, special drama or musical presentations, small groups, etc.
3. Meet with evangelism director at least quarterly to discuss and plan to cover the evangelism needs at upcoming church events.
4. Work with other ministry leaders to involve various ministries in evangelistic events and recruit volunteers from those ministries as needed.
5. Pray regularly for the evangelism ministry, for those who will attend special events, and for specific names of people needing salvation.
6. Be able to share your faith with others, using own life experiences and testimony as well as Scripture.

FUNERAL DINNER COORDINATOR

The funeral dinner coordinator is responsible for promptly coordinating funeral dinners for church members who lose a loved one. It is best if the person for this position does not hold a rigid, full-time job outside the home.

Ministry Area/Department	Outreach/Inreach
Position	Funeral dinner coordinator
Accountable To	Pastor or outreach director
Ministry Target	Grieving church members and families
Position Is	Volunteer
Position May Be Filled By	Church member
Minimum Maturity Level	New, growing Christian
Spiritual Gifts	Administration • Serving • Exhortation
Talents or Abilities Desired	Organizational skills • Good meal planner • Good motivator
Best Personality Traits	Expresser-analyst or dependable-leader
Passion For	Serving others in their time of need
Length of Service Commitment	One year minimum

ANTICIPATED TIME COMMITMENTS

1. **Doing ministry/preparing for ministry:** depending on need, may be zero hours some months and eight hours other months
2. **Participating in meetings/training:** as requested

RESPONSIBILITIES/DUTIES

1. Available for spur-of-the-moment ministry.
2. Plan well-rounded dinner for family on day of funeral.
3. Call family to arrange time and place of meal delivery and determine estimated number of family members who will attend.
4. Call funeral dinner helpers to help prepare meal and obtain disposable plates, napkins, forks, spoons, knives, cups, etc.
5. Coordinate delivery of meal to home, church or other location of family's choice.
6. Make sure dishes are returned to those who provided food.
7. Oversee budget and expenditures for the funeral dinner ministry.

FUNERAL DINNER HELPER

The funeral dinner helper is responsible for promptly cooking or contributing to funeral dinners for church members who lose a loved one. It is best if the person for this position does not hold a rigid, full-time job outside the home.

Ministry Area/Department	Outreach/Inreach
Position	Funeral dinner helper
Accountable To	Funeral dinner coordinator
Ministry Target	Grieving church members and families
Position Is	Volunteer
Position May Be Filled By	Church member
Minimum Maturity Level	New, growing Christian
Spiritual Gifts	Serving • Mercy-showing
Talents or Abilities Desired	Good cook
Best Personality Traits	Dependable-leader or dependable-expresser
Passion For	Cooking and serving others in their time of need
Length of Service Commitment	Two years minimum

ANTICIPATED TIME COMMITMENTS

1. **Doing ministry/preparing for ministry**: depending on need, may be zero hours some months and eight hours other months
2. **Participating in meetings/training**: minimal, as requested

RESPONSIBILITIES/DUTIES

1. Available for spur-of-the-moment ministry.
2. When called upon by funeral dinner coordinator, cook or contribute to a well-rounded dinner for families on day of funeral.
3. Sometimes run errands to obtain disposable plates, napkins, forks, spoons, knives, cups, etc.
4. Deliver food or utensils to home, church or location agreed upon with the funeral dinner coordinator.

HOMEBOUND/NURSING HOME MINISTER

The homebound/nursing home minister is responsible for regularly visiting church members and elderly community members to provide emotional encouragement and spiritual support.

Ministry Area/Department	Outreach/Inreach
Position	Homebound/nursing home minister
Accountable To	Homebound/nursing home ministry director
Ministry Target	Members and elderly community members
Position Is	Volunteer
Position May Be Filled By	Church member
Minimum Maturity Level	Stable, maturing Christian
Spiritual Gifts	Mercy-showing • Pastor/shepherd
Talents or Abilities Desired	Own transportation • Good listener • Able to pray with and for others • Must be able to commit to weekly ministry
Best Personality Traits	Dependable-leader or dependable-expresser • Compassionate • Encourager
Passion For	Ministering to the homebound and elderly
Length of Service Commitment	Two years minimum

ANTICIPATED TIME COMMITMENTS

1. **Doing ministry/preparing for ministry:** two hours a week
2. **Participating in meetings/training:** one hour a quarter

RESPONSIBILITIES/DUTIES

1. Participate in weekly visits to minister to homebound members and elderly community members in personal homes and nursing homes.
   a. Provide large-print inspirational reading material and Bibles, tapes of messages, video-tapes of special musicals to residents.
   b. Talk with, pray with, read to, listen to, play games with, go on walks with and otherwise assist residents as appropriate. The goal is to provide emotional encouragement and spiritual support.
   c. If musically talented, play musical instruments or provide special singing to entertain residents.
   d. Give cards, flowers, balloons, pictures, poems, lotion, tissues or other appropriate inexpensive items to residents on special occasions, such as birthdays and Christmas.
2. Inform the homebound/nursing-home ministry director of any special needs discovered in visiting homes/nursing homes.

HOMEBOUND/NURSING HOME MINISTRY DIRECTOR

The homebound/nursing home ministry director is responsible for organizing and overseeing the ministry of visiting and encouraging members and lonely community members who are homebound or living in nursing homes. Someone who does not work full-time or who is retired would be a great candidate for this ministry.

Ministry Area/Department	Outreach/Inreach
Position	Homebound/nursing home director
Accountable To	Shepherding pastor or outreach director
Ministry Target	Members and elderly community members
Position Is	Volunteer
Position May Be Filled By	Church member
Minimum Maturity Level	Stable, maturing Christian
Spiritual Gifts	Mercy-showing • Pastor/shepherd • Administration
Talents or Abilities Desired	Own transportation • Organizational skills • Good listener • Able to pray with and for others
Best Personality Traits	Dependable-leader or dependable-expresser • Compassionate • Encourager
Passion For	Ministering to the homebound and elderly
Length of Service Commitment	Two years minimum

ANTICIPATED TIME COMMITMENTS

1. **Doing ministry/preparing for ministry**: two hours a week
2. **Participating in meetings/training**: one hour a quarter

RESPONSIBILITIES/DUTIES

1. Maintain communication with shepherding pastor and outreach director to stay informed of additional ministry opportunities and to keep them abreast of the homebound/nursing home ministry progress.

2. Keep an up-to-date list of church members who are homebound—those who cannot attend church due to physical or mental health problems or long-term illness—or who are temporarily or permanently in a nursing home.

3. Contact local nursing homes to inform them of the church's nursing home ministry, introduce the church's nursing home ministers, and seek permission to visit residents who have no family or other regular visitors.

4. Provide training and instruction to homebound/nursing home ministers. The goal is to provide emotional encouragement and spiritual support. Ministers should:

    a. Provide large-print inspirational reading material and Bibles, tapes of messages, videotapes of special musicals for residents;

    b. Talk with, pray with, read to, listen to, play games with, go on walks with and otherwise assist residents as appropriate;

    c. If musically talented, play musical instruments and/or provide special singing to entertain residents.

5. Organize a weekly visitation schedule for the homebound/nursing-home ministers.

6. Inform shepherding pastor or appropriate church staff of special needs discovered in visiting homes/nursing homes.

HOSPITAL VISITATION COORDINATOR

The hospital visitation coordinator is responsible for making sure every hospitalized member or regular attendee is prayed for daily and visited by a hospital visitation minister.

Ministry Area/Department	Outreach/Inreach
Position	Hospital visitation coordinator
Accountable To	Shepherding pastor
Ministry Target	Members and regular attendees
Position Is	Volunteer
Position May Be Filled By	Church member
Minimum Maturity Level	Stable, maturing Christian
Spiritual Gifts	Mercy-showing • Pastor/shepherd • Administration
Talents or Abilities Desired	Own transportation • Good listener • Able to pray with and for others • Good organizational skills
Best Personality Traits	Dependable-leader or dependable-expresser • Compassionate • Encourager
Passion For	Comforting and cheering others
Length of Service Commitment	One year minimum

ANTICIPATED TIME COMMITMENTS

1. **Doing ministry/preparing for ministry**: depending on need, may be zero hours some months and eight hours other months
2. **Participating in meetings/training**: minimal, as requested

RESPONSIBILITIES/DUTIES

1. Maintain consistent contact with shepherding pastor and church office to stay informed of hospitalized people needing visits.
2. Contact hospital visitation ministers to inform them of hospitalizations, ask them to pray for special medical/spiritual needs and coordinate a visitation schedule for one of the ministers to visit each hospitalized person daily.
3. Participate in the hospital visitation program.
4. Inform shepherding pastor or appropriate church staff of special needs discovered in visiting the hospitalized.
5. Pray for hospitalized members and their families.

Hospital Visitation Minister

The hospital visitation minister is responsible for praying for and visiting hospitalized members or regular attendees.

Ministry Area/Department	Outreach/Inreach
Position	Hospital visitation minister
Accountable To	Hospital visitation coordinator
Ministry Target	Members and regular attendees
Position Is	Volunteer
Position May Be Filled By	Church member
Minimum Maturity Level	New, growing Christian
Spiritual Gifts	Mercy-showing • Pastor/shepherd
Talents or Abilities Desired	Own transportation • Good listener • Able to pray with and for others
Best Personality Traits	Dependable-leader or dependable-expresser • Compassionate • Encourager
Passion For	Comforting and cheering others
Length of Service Commitment	Two years minimum

Anticipated Time Commitments

1. **Doing ministry/preparing for ministry**: depending on need, may be zero hours some months and eight hours other months
2. **Participating in meetings/training**: minimal, as requested

Responsibilities/Duties

1. When hospital visitation coordinator informs you of hospitalizations, you will need to:
   a. Pray for special medical/spiritual needs;
   b. Participate in the visitation schedule for visiting each hospitalized person;
   c. When visiting, talk with and especially listen to the patient, pray with him or her and provide encouragement and cheer.
2. Inform hospital visitation coordinator of special needs discovered in visiting hospitalized members.

NEIGHBORHOOD FELLOWSHIP DIRECTOR

The neighborhood fellowship director is responsible for organizing and overseeing the neighborhood fellowship ministry to build a sense of community and support among church members and influence neighbors for Christ.

Ministry Area/Department	Outreach/Inreach
Position	Neighborhood fellowship director
Accountable To	Shepherding pastor or outreach director
Ministry Target	Church members and neighbors
Position Is	Volunteer
Position May Be Filled By	Church member
Minimum Maturity Level	Stable, maturing Christian
Spiritual Gifts	Pastor/shepherd • Exhortation • Administration
Talents or Abilities Desired	Good organizational skills
Best Personality Traits	Dependable • Expresser-leader or expresser-analyst
Passion For	Building a sense of community among church members and showing Christ's love to neighbors
Length of Service Commitment	Two years minimum

ANTICIPATED TIME COMMITMENTS
1. **Doing ministry/preparing for ministry:** two hours a week
2. **Participating in meetings/training:** one hour a quarter

RESPONSIBILITIES/DUTIES
1. Recruit and train couples as neighborhood fellowship group leaders.
2. Organize and plan the neighborhood fellowship program. Program should include regular neighborhood activities, devotional/prayer times, etc., with the goals of
   a. Ministering to church members;
   b. Building relationships with unchurched neighbors and influencing them for Christ.

NEIGHBORHOOD FELLOWSHIP GROUP LEADER

The neighborhood fellowship group leader is responsible for leading neighborhood fellowship ministry to build a sense of community and support among church members and influence neighbors for Christ. **Note**: A man and woman couple is preferred for leading the group in order to provide a sense of identity and common bond for both men and women in the group.

Ministry Area/Department	Outreach/Inreach
Position	Neighborhood fellowship group leader
Accountable To	Neighborhood fellowship director
Ministry Target	Church members and neighbors
Position Is	Volunteer
Position May Be Filled By	Church member
Minimum Maturity Level	Stable, maturing Christian
Spiritual Gifts	Pastor/shepherd • Exhortation • Teaching • Mercy-showing
Talents or Abilities Desired	Good communicator • Sensitive to other people's needs
Best Personality Traits	Expresser-leader
Passion For	Building a sense of community among church members and showing Christ's love to neighbors
Length of Service Commitment	One year minimum

ANTICIPATED TIME COMMITMENTS

1. **Doing ministry/preparing for ministry:** two hours a week
2. **Participating in meetings/training:** one hour a quarter

RESPONSIBILITIES/DUTIES

1. Meet with neighborhood fellowship director for training, brainstorming ideas, prayer and support.
2. Lead your own local neighborhood fellowship program in your home or local clubhouse. Program should include regular neighborhood activities, devotional/prayer times, etc. with the goals of:
   a. Ministering to church members.
   b. Building relationships with unchurched neighbors and influencing them for Christ.
3. Serve as a mentor and counselor to those in your neighborhood group. Seek advice from or refer others to appropriate professional counsel when necessary.

New Member Assimilator

The new member assimilator is responsible for welcoming new members, providing helpful information, helping them feel at home and bonding them to the church through relationships.

Ministry Area/Department	Outreach/Inreach
Position	New member assimilator
Accountable To	Shepherding pastors
Ministry Target	New church members
Position Is	Volunteer
Position May Be Filled By	Church member
Minimum Maturity Level	Stable, maturing Christian
Spiritual Gifts	Pastor/shepherd • Exhortation
Talents or Abilities Desired	Good communicator • Familiar with church facilities and ministries
Best Personality Traits	Dependable-expresser or dependable-leader
Passion For	Helping new members to feel at home in the church and motivating them to become involved
Length of Service Commitment	One year minimum

ANTICIPATED TIME COMMITMENTS

1. **Doing ministry/preparing for ministry:** one hour a week
2. **Participating in meetings/training:** one yearly training meeting or as requested

RESPONSIBILITIES/DUTIES

1. Greet and welcome new members after worship services.
2. Become familiar with the church facilities. Show new members around the church facilities.
3. Enroll new members in the new members class and inform them of the church's ministries and classes/small groups that may apply to or interest them.
4. Be aware of the church's ministries. Answer new members' questions regarding ministry opportunities available.
5. Introduce new members to current members—especially those who may have common interests/family life/ages, etc.
6. Make a point to greet new members every week for at least the first six weeks.

Outreach Director

The outreach director will organize and oversee the outreach ministries of the church, including evaluating and planning for the future.

Ministry Area/Department	Outreach/Inreach
Position	Outreach director
Accountable To	Executive pastor or pastor
Ministry Target	Community and families of church members
Position Is	Volunteer
Position May Be Filled By	Church member
Minimum Maturity Level	Stable, maturing Christian
Spiritual Gifts	Evangelism • Pastor/shepherd • Exhortation • Teaching
Talents or Abilities Desired	Good communicator • Motivator
Best Personality Traits	Expresser-leader or analyst-expresser
Passion For	Reaching people at their point of need and leading them to a personal relationship with Christ
Length of Service Commitment	Two years minimum

Anticipated Time Commitments

1. **Doing ministry/preparing for ministry:** three to four hours a week
2. **Participating in meetings/training:** one hour a month

Responsibilities/Duties

1. Organize and oversee the outreach ministries of the church.
2. Recruit and train leaders for the various outreach ministries.
3. Research, survey and evaluate the church and community to determine what outreach ministries are most needed and if existing ministries are effective.
4. Develop new ministries as needed.
5. Obtain and supply materials needed for the outreach ministries.
6. Meet with leaders of outreach ministries quarterly to get a report on the ministry progress, to brainstorm, to determine how to improve the ministries and to discuss challenges and solutions.
7. Act as a liaison between outreach ministry leaders and the pastor.
8. Work with public relations director to promote a positive image of the church in the community while reaching out to community members.
9. Pray regularly for the outreach ministries.

10. Promptly give church visitor information to visitor follow-up assistants for follow-up calls, letters and visits.

11. Oversee budget and expenditures for the outreach ministry.

PANTRY ORGANIZER

The pantry organizer will organize and maintain the pantry of clothing and nonperishable food for benevolent use.

Ministry Area/Department	Outreach/Inreach
Position	Pantry organizer
Accountable To	Outreach director
Ministry Target	Needy church and community members
Position Is	Volunteer
Position May Be Filled By	Church member
Minimum Maturity Level	New, growing Christian
Spiritual Gifts	Serving • Mercy-showing • Administration
Talents or Abilities Desired	Organizer • Self-motivated • Doesn't mind working alone, but works well with others
Best Personality Traits	Leader-analyst or analyst-dependable
Passion For	Organizing things and helping those in need
Length of Service Commitment	One year minimum

ANTICIPATED TIME COMMITMENTS

1. **Doing ministry/preparing for ministry**: one hour a week—occasionally more
2. **Participating in meetings/training**: minimal, as requested

RESPONSIBILITIES/DUTIES

1. Organize the pantry which includes clothing and nonperishable foods: canned, boxed, bagged, dried, etc.
   a. Sort and shelve foods according to like kind. Dispose of any outdated goods.
   b. Sort and hang or shelve clothing according to size, type and whether for male or female. Only accept clean clothing in good condition. Dispose of worn-out clothing. Have volunteer seamstresses make minor repairs such as replacing buttons or stitching hems.
2. Schedule appointments for benevolence ministers or people referred for assistance to pick up items from the pantry.
3. Prepare items for pickup or assist with selection of needed items.
4. Let outreach director or benevolence ministers know when supplies are low so an announcement can be made at services and in newsletter asking for donations of items or money.
5. Receive and process new donations.

PRISON MINISTER

The prison minister will assist the prison ministry director in reaching out and ministering to local jail or prison inmates and families.

Ministry Area/Department	Outreach/Inreach
Position	Prison minister
Accountable To	Prison ministry director
Ministry Target	Prisoners and their families
Position Is	Volunteer
Position May Be Filled By	Church member
Minimum Maturity Level	Stable, maturing Christian
Spiritual Gifts	Evangelism • Pastor/shepherd • Teaching
Talents or Abilities Desired	Good communicator
Best Personality Traits	Expresser-leader • Dependable
Passion For	Reaching people at their point of need and showing them the love of Christ
Length of Service Commitment	One year minimum

ANTICIPATED TIME COMMITMENTS

1. **Doing ministry/preparing for ministry**: three hours a week
2. **Participating in meetings/training**: one hour a month

RESPONSIBILITIES/DUTIES

1. Assist the prison ministry director in conducting a weekly Bible study and devotional time at the jail or prison for those prisoners who are allowed to attend.
2. Provide spiritual counseling and reading materials for those who are interested.
3. Visit the families of prisoners who become Christians to inform and minister to them. Encourage them to become involved in a local church.
4. Minister to the families by providing physical help. These families often experience hardships due to a parent/spouse in jail or prison.
   a. Deliver food and/or clothing from the church benevolence ministry.
   b. Help with home repairs.
   c. Contact Big Buddy coordinator to find a Big Buddy for the prisoner's children to provide a male or female mentor while the parent is away.
5. Pray regularly for the prison ministry and those who will be touched by it.
6. Consider volunteering to teach special classes to the men or women on topics such as preparing for job interviews, parenting, building healthy family relationships or tutoring them in subjects such as reading, language skills, etc. Obtain approval from the proper authorities.

PRISON MINISTRY DIRECTOR

The prison ministry director will organize and oversee the prison ministry to local jail or prison inmates and families.

Ministry Area/Department	Outreach/Inreach
Position	Prison ministry director
Accountable To	Outreach director
Ministry Target	Prisoners and their families
Position Is	Volunteer
Position May Be Filled By	Church member
Minimum Maturity Level	Stable, maturing Christian
Spiritual Gifts	Evangelism • Pastor/shepherd • Teaching
Talents or Abilities Desired	Good communicator • Good organizational skills
Best Personality Traits	Expresser-leader • Dependable
Passion For	Reaching people at their point of need and leading them to a personal relationship with Christ
Length of Service Commitment	Two years minimum

ANTICIPATED TIME COMMITMENTS

1. **Doing ministry/preparing for ministry:** three hours a week
2. **Participating in meetings/training:** one hour a month

RESPONSIBILITIES/DUTIES

1. Organize and oversee the prison ministry.
2. Recruit and train prison ministers to assist you.
3. Contact your local jail and/or prison authorities and/or chaplains to explain your ministry and seek permission to minister in their facilities.
4. Conduct a weekly Bible study and devotional time at the jail or prison for those prisoners who are allowed and desire to attend.
5. Provide spiritual counseling and reading materials for those who are interested.
6. Visit the families of prisoners who become Christians to share what has happened and to minister to them. Encourage them to become involved in a local church.
7. Minister to the families by providing physical help since these families often experience hardships due to a parent/spouse being in jail or prison.
   a. Seek assistance from church benevolence fund or pantry.
   b. Receive special offerings and donations for specific needs.
   c. Seek volunteers to help with home repairs.

d. If church has a Big Buddy program or if prison ministers will serve, pair Big Buddies with the prisoner's children to help provide a male or female mentor while the parent is away.

8. Pray regularly for the prison ministry and those involved.

9. Oversee budget and expenditures for the prison ministry.

SHEPHERDING PASTOR

The shepherding pastor will assist the pastor in exhorting the saints, providing spiritual nurture and equipping members for ministry.

Ministry Area/Department	Outreach/Inreach
Position	Shepherding pastor
Accountable To	Pastor
Ministry Target	Congregation
Position Is	Paid staff
Position May Be Filled By	Church member
Minimum Maturity Level	Stable, maturing Christian
Spiritual Gifts	Pastor/shepherd • Exhortation • Teaching
Talents or Abilities Desired	Experience in counseling • Communicates well • Agrees with church doctrine • Has firm foundation in biblical studies • Good leadership skills
Best Personality Traits	Expresser-leader or dependable-expresser • Compassionate • Understanding
Passion For	Nurturing church members
Length of Service Commitment	Three years

ANTICIPATED TIME COMMITMENTS

1. **Doing ministry/preparing for ministry:** eight hours a week
2. **Participating in meetings/training:** one hour a week

RESPONSIBILITIES/DUTIES

1. Greet people before and after services.
2. Schedule at least four 30- to 45-minute visits per week with church members for the purpose of:
   a. Getting to know members;
   b. Offering prayer and spiritual nurturing, plus encouragement to be faithful in attendance, personal devotions, family devotions, ministry in the church, etc.;
   c. Answering questions about the church and spiritual matters.
3. Make emergency visits to support members facing a death, hospitalization in an emergency or in other crucial circumstances.
4. Conduct a limited number of counseling appointments with church members.
5. Report special or critical needs to the pastor.
6. Pray regularly for church members and leaders.

SPECIAL EVENTS OFFICE VOLUNTEER

The special events office volunteer will assist with any additional office work created by special outreach events.

Ministry Area/Department	Outreach/Inreach
Position	Special events office volunteer
Accountable To	Outreach ministry director
Ministry Target	Congregation and community
Position Is	Volunteer
Position May Be Filled By	Church member
Minimum Maturity Level	New, growing Christian
Spiritual Gifts	Serving • Administration
Talents or Abilities Desired	Typing/computer experience • Preparing flyers for mailing • Experience handling business phones
Best Personality Traits	Analyst-dependable
Passion For	Supporting special projects through behind-the-scenes work
Length of Service Commitment	One year minimum

ANTICIPATED TIME COMMITMENTS

1. **Doing ministry/preparing for ministry**: varies, up to eight hours a week preceding special event
2. **Participating in meetings/training**: as requested

RESPONSIBILITIES/DUTIES

1. Prepare promotional material for distribution or display.
2. Prepare mailings; may include folding flyers, collating pages, addressing and stuffing envelopes, applying postage, etc.
3. Make phone calls—reminder calls to members, following up on printing or other special jobs.
4. Other tasks as needed.

Sports Team Shepherd

The sports team shepherd will build relationships with sports team members, their friends and their families. The main goals are to encourage noninvolved Christians to become active and to lead non-Christians to a personal relationship with Jesus Christ.

Ministry Area/Department	Outreach/Inreach
Position	Sports team shepherd
Accountable To	Outreach director
Ministry Target	Sports team players and families
Position Is	Volunteer
Position May Be Filled By	Church member
Minimum Maturity Level	Stable, maturing Christian
Spiritual Gifts	Evangelism • Pastor/shepherd • Exhortation
Talents or Abilities Desired	Good communicator
Best Personality Traits	Expresser-leader • Dependable
Passion For	Building relationships and sharing Christ
Length of Service Commitment	One season

Anticipated Time Commitments

1. **Doing ministry/preparing for ministry**: three hours a week during sports season
2. **Participating in meetings/training**: one hour a year

Responsibilities/Duties

1. Assist the coach in ministry opportunities during the sports season.
2. Mingle with players and their friends and families in order to:
   a. Build positive relationships.
   b. Encourage inactive members to become involved in ministries that fit their interests and spiritual gifts.
   c. Invite nonmembers to other church activities and services with the ultimate goal of leading them to Jesus Christ as Lord and Savior and to fellowship with the Body of Christ—or to become active in worship and ministry if already a Christian.

SUPPORT GROUP DIRECTOR

The support group director will coordinate and oversee the support group ministry. This will involve determining the need for specific groups, recruiting and training volunteers, obtaining materials as needed and promoting the ministry.

Ministry Area/Department	General administration
Position	Support group director
Accountable To	Outreach director
Ministry Target	Congregation and community
Position Is	Volunteer
Position May Be Filled By	Church member
Minimum Maturity Level	Stable, maturing Christian
Spiritual Gifts	Administration • Exhortation • Mercy-showing • Pastor/shepherd
Talents or Abilities Desired	Good organizational skills
Best Personality Traits	Compassionate • Leader-dependable or analyst-leader
Passion For	Reaching and nurturing people at their point of need
Length of Service Commitment	Two years minimum

ANTICIPATED TIME COMMITMENTS

1. **Doing ministry/preparing for ministry:** one hour a week
2. **Participating in meetings/training:** two hours a quarter or as needed

RESPONSIBILITIES/DUTIES

1. Coordinate volunteers to serve as support-group facilitators.
2. Develop and implement a training program for support-group facilitators.
3. Review curricula and recommended resources available for various support groups.
4. Order and provide support-group materials for group facilitators.
5. Recognize, encourage and motivate group facilitators.
6. Serve as a liaison between support groups and pastor.
7. Research and determine need of and resources available for specific support groups.
8. Oversee budget and expenditures for the support-group ministry.

SUPPORT GROUP FACILITATOR

The support group facilitator will lead a specific support group which he or she has a special burden for or understanding of because of training or life experience. This person will lead the Bible study and provide spiritual and emotional support in the small support-group environment.

Ministry Area/Department	General outreach
Position	Support group facilitator
Accountable To	Support group director
Ministry Target	Congregation and community
Position Is	Volunteer
Position May Be Filled By	Church member
Minimum Maturity Level	Stable, maturing Christian
Spiritual Gifts	Exhortation • Mercy-showing • Pastor/shepherd
Talents or Abilities Desired	Communicator • Leader • Student of God's Word
Best Personality Traits	Compassionate but firm • Expresser-analyst or expresser-leader
Passion For	Reaching and nurturing people at their point of need
Length of Service Commitment	Three to six months

ANTICIPATED TIME COMMITMENTS

1. **Doing ministry/preparing for ministry:** three to four hours a week
2. **Participating in meetings/training:** one hour a quarter or as needed

RESPONSIBILITIES/DUTIES

1. Provide encouragement to people within the support group.
2. Lead in Bible study and discussion of material related to special needs of support group.
3. Pray with and for people in support group.
4. Report any problems or special needs to the support-group director.
5. Plan at least one social activity for the support-group participants. If only one social, have it at or near the end of a particular study.

VISITOR FOLLOW-UP ASSISTANT

The visitor follow-up assistant is a role two people will fill together. They will visit people who have visited the church's services or special events and requested a visit. These volunteers will represent Christ and the church and must conduct themselves in such a manner as to positively influence others.

Ministry Area/Department	Outreach/Inreach
Position	Visitor follow-up assistant
Accountable To	Outreach director
Ministry Target	Visitors
Position Is	Volunteer
Position May Be Filled By	Church member
Minimum Maturity Level	Stable, maturing Christian paired with a new, growing Christian
Spiritual Gifts	Evangelism • Exhortation • Pastor/shepherd
Talents or Abilities Desired	Good communicator • Well groomed
Best Personality Traits	Expresser • Dependable
Passion For	Making people feel important • Building relationships • Sharing Christ
Length of Service Commitment	One year minimum

ANTICIPATED TIME COMMITMENTS

1. **Doing ministry/preparing for ministry**: one hour a week
2. **Participating in meetings/training**: one hour a year

RESPONSIBILITIES/DUTIES

1. Be familiar with church ministries and opportunities.
2. Visit people who have visited church services and requested a visit. Information will be provided by the outreach director. Be prepared to:
   a. Pray with them.
   b. Answer questions regarding the church's ministries; take a brochure, if available.
   c. Give spiritual guidance; refer more serious issues to pastor or appropriate, qualified counselor.
   d. Lead them to Christ.
   e. Encourage them to get involved with the new members' class, small groups, etc.
   f. Pray before every visit.
3. After visits, pray for those who need to make decisions or who made decisions during your visit.

VISITOR FOLLOW-UP CALLER

The visitor follow-up caller will call people who have visited the church's services or special events to make them feel welcome, answer questions regarding the church ministries and invite them to return.

Ministry Area/Department	Outreach/Inreach
Position	Visitor follow-up caller
Accountable To	Outreach director
Ministry Target	Visitors
Position Is	Volunteer
Position May Be Filled By	Church member
Minimum Maturity Level	New, growing Christian
Spiritual Gifts	Evangelism • Exhortation • Pastor/shepherd
Talents or Abilities Desired	Pleasant voice • Clear speech
Best Personality Traits	Dependable-expresser
Passion For	Making people feel important, building relationships and sharing Christ
Length of Service Commitment	One year minimum

ANTICIPATED TIME COMMITMENTS

1. **Doing ministry/preparing for ministry:** one hour a week
2. **Participating in meetings/training:** one hour a year

RESPONSIBILITIES/DUTIES

1. Be familiar with church ministries and opportunities.
2. Call people who have visited church services or events to thank them for coming, ask if they have any questions about the church ministries or would like someone from church to visit them, and invite them to return again. This call should be made within three days of the visitors' attendance at the church service or event. Visitor information will be provided by the outreach director.

VISITOR FOLLOW-UP WRITER

The visitor follow-up writer will send a welcome letter to every first-time visitor to the church's services or special events.

Ministry Area/Department	Outreach/Inreach
Position	Visitor follow-up writer
Accountable To	Outreach director
Ministry Target	Visitors
Position Is	Volunteer
Position May Be Filled By	Church member
Minimum Maturity Level	New, growing Christian
Spiritual Gifts	Exhortation • Pastor/shepherd
Talents or Abilities Desired	Good penmanship or typing skills
Best Personality Traits	Analyst • Expresser
Passion For	Making people feel important • Building relationships • Sharing Christ
Length of Service Commitment	One year minimum

ANTICIPATED TIME COMMITMENTS

1. **Doing ministry/preparing for ministry:** one hour a week
2. **Participating in meetings/training:** one hour a year

RESPONSIBILITIES/DUTIES

1. Be familiar with church ministries and opportunities.
2. Send a follow-up letter to everyone who visits the church. Information will be provided by the outreach director. The purpose of the letter is to:
   a. Welcome them to the church and thank them for visiting.
   b. Tell them about upcoming special events, sermon or lesson series, etc.
   c. Invite them to come again.
3. Pray for every person to whom you mail a letter.

PRAYER

COTTAGE PRAYER LEADER

The cottage prayer leader will host a group prayer meeting in his or her home once a month.

Ministry Area/Department	Prayer
Position	Cottage prayer leader
Accountable To	Prayer ministry coordinator
Ministry Target	Individuals, church, community, nation, world, special crusades/events
Position Is	Volunteer
Position May Be Filled By	Church member
Minimum Maturity Level	New, growing Christian
Spiritual Gifts	Pastor/shepherd • Exhortation
Talents or Abilities Desired	Able to host monthly group prayer meetings in the home
Best Personality Traits	Expresser-leader
Passion For	Spending time with God in prayer • Petitioning God on the behalf of others
Length of Service Commitment	One year minimum

ANTICIPATED TIME COMMITMENTS

1. **Doing ministry/preparing for ministry:** one to two hours a month
2. **Participating in meetings/training:** one hour a quarter

RESPONSIBILITIES/DUTIES

1. Open your home to a group prayer meeting (thus the name "cottage prayer meeting") at least once a month. Meetings will be held weekly and will rotate to different locations.
2. Schedule dates for hosting the cottage prayer meeting at your home (arrange through the prayer ministry director).
3. Greet the prayer group, have a brief Scripture reading and/or devotional, begin prayer.
4. Invite the group to share answers to prayer.
5. Optional: Have simple refreshments and brief time of fellowship.

PRAYER CHAIN LINK

The prayer chain link will keep the prayer chain strong by praying for emergency requests as they arise and contacting the appropriate person in the prayer chain for additional prayer support.

Ministry Area/Department	Prayer
Position	Prayer chain link
Accountable To	Prayer ministry coordinator
Ministry Target	Congregation and its friends and families
Position Is	Volunteer
Position May Be Filled By	Church member
Minimum Maturity Level	New, growing Christian
Spiritual Gifts	Pastor/shepherd • Mercy-showing
Talents or Abilities Desired	Accessible by telephone • Available every day
Best Personality Traits	Dependable-leader or dependable-expresser • Discreet • Trustworthy
Passion For	Interceding to God on behalf of others in times of great need
Length of Service Commitment	One year minimum

ANTICIPATED TIME COMMITMENTS

1. **Doing ministry/preparing for ministry**: up to one hour a week
2. **Participating in meetings/training**: as requested

RESPONSIBILITIES/DUTIES

1. Be easily accessible by phone.
2. Pray for emergency prayer requests upon hearing of the needs and continue to remember the needs in prayer for as long as necessary.
3. Call next person in the prayer chain to pass on the emergency prayer request.
4. Do not share confidential information with those outside the prayer chain and do not gossip about the special needs.

PRAYER MINISTRY COORDINATOR

The prayer ministry coordinator will organize and oversee the church prayer ministries.

Ministry Area/Department	Prayer
Position	Prayer ministry coordinator
Accountable To	Pastor or shepherding pastor
Ministry Target	Congregation and its friends and families
Position Is	Volunteer
Position May Be Filled By	Church member
Minimum Maturity Level	Stable, maturing Christian
Spiritual Gifts	Pastor/shepherd • Administration • Mercy-showing • Exhortation
Talents or Abilities Desired	Accessible by telephone • Available every day • Strong belief in the power of prayer
Best Personality Traits	Leader-dependable • Expresser • Discreet • Trustworthy
Passion For	Praying and exhorting others to spend time in prayer
Length of Service Commitment	One year minimum

ANTICIPATED TIME COMMITMENTS

1. **Doing ministry/preparing for ministry**: one to two hours a week
2. **Participating in meetings/training**: one hour a month

RESPONSIBILITIES/DUTIES

1. Organize and oversee the church prayer ministries.
    a. Recruit leaders and develop the schedule for cottage prayer meetings.
    b. Recruit participants and organize a contact list for the prayer chain for emergency requests.
    c. Develop a rotation schedule for prayer warriors to pray during services and special events.
    d. Contact appropriate leaders to share praises and prayer requests.
2. Be available daily to receive and distribute requests to the appropriate prayer ministry leaders in a timely manner: first link in the prayer chain, a prayer warrior or cottage prayer leader.
3. Provide a phone number for contact in case of emergency requests.
4. Pray for every request you receive.
5. Oversee budget and expenditures for the prayer ministry.

PRAYER WARRIOR

The prayer warrior will pray continually and consistently for a great variety of needs.

Ministry Area/Department	Prayer
Position	Prayer warrior
Accountable To	Prayer ministry coordinator
Ministry Target	Individuals, church, community, nation and world
Position Is	Volunteer
Position May Be Filled By	Church member
Minimum Maturity Level	New, growing Christian and mature Christians
Spiritual Gifts	Pastor/shepherd • Mercy-showing • Evangelism
Talents or Abilities Desired	Available to spend much time in prayer • Able to pray alone or with groups
Best Personality Traits	Leader-dependable • Discreet • Trustworthy
Passion For	Spending great amounts of time with God in prayer • Petitioning God on the behalf of people with great needs
Length of Service Commitment	One year minimum

ANTICIPATED TIME COMMITMENTS

1. **Doing ministry/preparing for ministry:** four hours minimum a week
2. **Participating in meetings/training:** as requested

RESPONSIBILITIES/DUTIES

1. Be easily accessible by phone.
2. Pray for emergency prayer requests.
3. Pray for needs such as salvation, commitment and rededicated lives, protection from evil, wisdom and safety for leaders, special requests, to tear down strongholds, etc.
4. Pray for local, national and international concerns, including missions.
5. Pray during church services, weekly prayer meetings and at home.
6. Do not share confidential information with those outside the prayer ministry and do not gossip about the special needs.

SENIOR ADULTS

SENIOR ADULT ACTIVITIES COORDINATOR

The senior adult activities coordinator will plan and organize one special activity a month for senior adults to promote ministry to one another and include fun, fellowship and encouragement.

Ministry Area/Department	Senior adults
Position	Activities coordinator
Accountable To	Senior adult pastor
Ministry Target	Senior adults
Position Is	Volunteer
Position May Be Filled By	Church member
Minimum Maturity Level	New, growing Christian
Spiritual Gifts	Administration • Exhortation
Talents or Abilities Desired	Good physical health • Planning and organizational skills
Best Personality Traits	Leader-dependable
Passion For	Planning activities for fun and fellowship
Length of Service Commitment	One year minimum

ANTICIPATED TIME COMMITMENTS

1. **Doing ministry/preparing for ministry**: one hour a week
2. **Participating in meetings/training**: one hour a quarter

RESPONSIBILITIES/DUTIES

1. Get to know the senior adults in the church and find out what their interests are and what activities they enjoy. Do a yearly survey regarding activity choices.
2. Plan and organize a monthly activity for senior adults.
   a. Consider the interests and activities enjoyed by senior adults.
   b. Occasionally try something new for variety and excitement.
   c. Schedule some activities in the church facilities and others in different locations—even short day trips.
   d. Research—other churches, books, etc.—to discover what other senior adult ministries are doing.
3. Prepare an activity calendar and distribute copies to senior adults.
4. Give a copy of the activity schedule to the administrative secretary for when someone calls with questions about dates and activities and so that the information may be included in the church master calendar.

SENIOR ADULT BIBLE STUDY ASSISTANT

The senior adult Bible study assistant is the right arm of the senior adult Bible study teacher. The assistant must be prepared to fill in for the teacher when necessary, assist with keeping watch over the flock and coordinating class leaders and functions. The assistant is expected to teach, reach and minister to members and prospects under the direction of the teacher.

Ministry Area/Department	Senior adult Sunday School
Position	Senior adult Bible study assistant
Accountable To	Senior adult Bible study teacher
Ministry Target	Senior adults
Position Is	Volunteer
Position May Be Filled By	Church member
Minimum Maturity Level	Stable, maturing Christian
Spiritual Gifts	Shepherd • Teaching • Exhortation
Talents or Abilities Desired	Communicator • Comfortable speaking to groups • Able to allow someone else to lead but willing to take the lead when necessary
Best Personality Traits	Dependable-leader
Passion For	Discipling senior adults and providing support for other leaders
Length of Service Commitment	One year minimum

ANTICIPATED TIME COMMITMENTS
1. **Doing ministry/preparing for ministry:** one to two hours a week
2. **Participating in meetings/training:** one hour a month

RESPONSIBILITIES/DUTIES
1. Participate in teacher meetings and training opportunities.
2. Study each weekly lesson and be available to lead the class in the senior adult Bible study teacher's absence.
3. Pray for class members/visitors.
4. Promote spiritual growth and unity among class members.

SENIOR ADULT BIBLE STUDY TEACHER

The senior adult Bible study teacher is the shepherd of the class and is responsible for overseeing or coordinating all class leaders and functions. The teacher is expected to teach, reach and minister to members and prospects with the help of other leaders within the class.

Ministry Area/Department	Senior adult Sunday School
Position	Senior adult Bible study teacher
Accountable To	Sunday School director
Ministry Target	Senior adults
Position Is	Volunteer
Position May Be Filled By	Church member
Minimum Maturity Level	Stable, maturing Christian
Spiritual Gifts	Shepherding • Teaching • Exhortation
Talents or Abilities Desired	Communicator • Comfortable speaking to groups
Best Personality Traits	Dependable-leader • Expresser
Passion For	Discipling senior adults
Length of Service Commitment	One year minimum

ANTICIPATED TIME COMMITMENTS

1. **Doing ministry/preparing for ministry:** three hours a week
2. **Participating in meetings/training:** one hour a month

RESPONSIBILITIES/DUTIES

1. Participate in teacher meetings and training opportunities.
2. Work with Sunday School director to choose curriculum for the class.
3. Study and prepare for each weekly lesson.
4. Pray for class members and visitors.
5. Arrive 15 minutes before class begins to make sure classroom is prepared and to greet people as they arrive.
6. Lead class each week and involve participants in studying and learning God's Word through various teaching methods.
7. Promote spiritual growth and unity among class members.
8. Organize class into care groups of six people or less with one leader per group.

SENIOR ADULT CARE GROUP LEADER

The senior adult care group leader is responsible for showing Christian love and concern to a small group of fellow senior adults through maintaining regular contact and encouragement.

Ministry Area/Department	Senior adults
Position	Senior adult care group leader
Accountable To	Senior adult pastor
Ministry Target	Senior adults
Position Is	Volunteer
Position May Be Filled By	Church member
Minimum Maturity Level	New, growing Christian
Spiritual Gifts	Pastor/shepherd • Mercy-showing • Exhortation
Talents or Abilities Desired	Concern for others • Accessible by telephone • Able to write and mail brief notes and cards
Best Personality Traits	Dependable-expresser • Expresser-analyst • Compassionate
Passion For	Spiritual and physical well-being of fellow Christians
Length of Service Commitment	One year minimum

ANTICIPATED TIME COMMITMENTS

1. **Doing ministry/preparing for ministry:** one hour a week
2. **Participating in meetings/training:** as requested

RESPONSIBILITIES/DUTIES

Responsible for caring for a small group of senior saints.

a. Pray for the people in your care group.

b. Send cards when appropriate: birthday, thinking of you, get well, sympathy, etc.

c. Call periodically to touch base with each person in your care group.

d. Call to check on those who are absent to let them know they were missed and to make sure they are all right.

e. With person's permission, pass on any special prayer requests to senior adult class prayer leader, senior adult pastor and appropriate class teacher.

f. Notify proper minister or authorities if one of your care group members has an emergency or critical need for assistance.

Senior Adult Class Fellowship Leader

The senior adult class fellowship leader is responsible for planning and coordinating all class social events at church or elsewhere and for recruiting class members to help as needed. This leader will promote unity among the group.

Ministry Area/Department	Senior adult Sunday school
Position	Senior adult class fellowship leader
Accountable To	Senior adult Bible study teacher
Ministry Target	Senior adults
Position Is	Volunteer
Position May Be Filled By	Church member
Minimum Maturity Level	New, growing Christian
Spiritual Gifts	Administration • Serving • Exhortation
Talents or Abilities Desired	Organizer • Motivator
Best Personality Traits	Expresser-dependable • Sociable
Passion For	Planning and orchestrating experiences that build relationships and encourage others
Length of Service Commitment	One year minimum

Anticipated Time Commitments

1. **Doing ministry/preparing for ministry:** one hour a month
2. **Participating in meetings/training:** one hour a quarter

Responsibilities/Duties

1. Participate in training opportunities.
2. Plan, coordinate and lead class social events.
3. Encourage get-acquainted or icebreaker activities within the class.
4. Plan for occasional—or even weekly—refreshments before class.

SENIOR ADULT CLASS OUTREACH LEADER

The senior adult class outreach leader is the reaching arm of the class. This person is responsible for contacting and beginning relationships with prospects, visitors and new members in order to point them to Christ and assimilate them into the church through the Sunday School or other Bible-study groups.

Ministry Area/Department	Senior adult Sunday School
Position	Senior adult class outreach leader
Accountable To	Senior adult Bible study teacher
Ministry Target	Senior adults
Position Is	Volunteer
Position May Be Filled By	Church member
Minimum Maturity Level	Stable, maturing Christian
Spiritual Gifts	Evangelism • Administration • Exhortation
Talents or Abilities Desired	Good communicator • Good organizational skills
Best Personality Traits	Expresser-leader • Outgoing
Passion For	Influencing other senior adults for Christ and encouraging them to become involved in the local church
Length of Service Commitment	One year minimum

ANTICIPATED TIME COMMITMENTS
1. **Doing ministry/preparing for ministry:** one hour a week
2. **Participating in meetings/training:** one hour a month

RESPONSIBILITIES/DUTIES
1. Participate in training opportunities.
2. Coordinate efforts with church outreach director and inform him or her of visitation progress.
3. Work with class members to identify, witness to and minister to prospects and enroll new members.
4. Develop a class prospect file and keep a record of contacts with those prospects and the results.
5. Pray for prospects, visitors and new members.
6. Initiate follow-up contacts with class visitors: phone, write, visit.
7. Contact prospects to inform them of the class studies, activities, etc. and invite them to participate: phone, write, visit.
8. Be prepared to lead prospects to Christ or to provide a counselor when needed.
9. Welcome visitors and help new members feel accepted; introduce them to others, assimilating them into the life of the church.

SENIOR ADULT CLASS PRAYER LEADER

The senior adult class prayer leader is responsible for praying fervently, organizing and leading a class prayer chain and encouraging spiritual growth in class members through daily devotions and prayer.

Ministry Area/Department	Senior adult Sunday School
Position	Senior adult class prayer leader
Accountable To	Senior adult Bible study teacher
Ministry Target	Senior adults
Position Is	Volunteer
Position May Be Filled By	Church member
Minimum Maturity Level	Stable, maturing Christian
Spiritual Gifts	Mercy-showing • Pastor/shepherd • Exhortation
Talents or Abilities Desired	Good communicator • Good listener • Willing to spend time in prayer
Best Personality Traits	Expresser-analyst • Caring • Serious • Discreet
Passion For	Interceding for others in prayer • Belief in the power of prayer
Length of Service Commitment	One year minimum

ANTICIPATED TIME COMMITMENTS

1. **Doing ministry/preparing for ministry**: three hours a week
2. **Participating in meetings/training**: one hour a week (prayer meeting)

RESPONSIBILITIES/DUTIES

1. Pray daily for the needs of members, prospects and for church activities, ministries and leaders.
2. Organize a class prayer chain through the care-group leaders to inform class members of special or urgent prayer needs.
3. Encourage class members to pray for foreign and home missions.
4. Provide or recommend devotional material and exhort members to have daily devotions.

SENIOR ADULT CLASS SECRETARY

The senior adult class secretary is responsible for keeping accurate, up-to-date records; seeing that appropriate forms are completed regarding enrollment changes, visitors, etc.; preparing or assisting with class correspondence when needed; and welcoming newcomers to the class.

Ministry Area/Department	Senior adult Sunday School
Position	Senior adult class secretary
Accountable To	Senior adult Bible study teacher
Ministry Target	Senior adults
Position Is	Volunteer
Position May Be Filled By	Church member
Minimum Maturity Level	New, growing Christian
Spiritual Gifts	Administration • Serving
Talents or Abilities Desired	Organized • Detail oriented • Good penmanship
Best Personality Traits	Dependable-analyst • Friendly
Passion For	Organization, accuracy and serving as a support person
Length of Service Commitment	One year minimum

ANTICIPATED TIME COMMITMENTS

1. **Doing ministry/preparing for ministry:** one hour a week
2. **Participating in meetings/training:** yearly training workshop

RESPONSIBILITIES/DUTIES

1. Participate in training opportunities, yearly or as presented.
2. Keep accurate records of member attendance and up-to-date personal information—address, phone, birthday, etc.
3. Welcome visitors and help new members feel accepted.
4. Ask visitors to complete appropriate forms or personally register them by obtaining names, addresses and phone numbers; determine whether or not they are a member of another church.
5. Keep records of visitor and prospect information for outreach purposes. Have this information readily available to the senior adult Bible-study teacher, outreach leader and other concerned staff.
6. Complete weekly attendance form, collect class offerings and turn them in to senior adult records clerk.
7. Prepare or assist with special correspondence to class members.

SENIOR ADULT GUEST FOLLOW-UP ASSISTANT

The senior adult guest follow-up assistant will follow up every senior adult guest who visits the church. This involves phone calls, visits and cards to make the guests feel welcome and cared for.

Ministry Area/Department	Senior adults
Position	Senior adult guest follow-up assistant
Accountable To	Senior adult outreach director
Ministry Target	Senior adult guests
Position Is	Volunteer
Position May Be Filled By	Church member
Minimum Maturity Level	New, growing Christian, paired with stable, maturing Christian when visiting
Spiritual Gifts	Mercy-showing • Pastor/shepherd
Talents or Abilities Desired	Accessible by telephone • Able to write and mail brief notes and cards
Best Personality Traits	Dependable-analyst • Friendly • Compassionate
Passion For	Influencing people for Christ and the church
Length of Service Commitment	Two years minimum

ANTICIPATED TIME COMMITMENTS

1. **Doing ministry/preparing for ministry**: one hour a week
2. **Participating in meetings/training**: minimal, as requested

RESPONSIBILITIES/DUTIES

1. Contact all senior adult guests who have attended your class or the church.
2. Extend a warm welcome, a hand of fellowship and a note of appreciation or encouragement with the goal of helping the guest feel welcome and influencing him or her to visit again and become committed to Christ and the church.
   a. Phone within 24 hours of visiting class, service or activity. Ask if it's all right to schedule a brief visit.
   b. Visit within a week if guest approved or requested a visit. Plan to keep the visit brief, unless the guest asks you to stay longer.
   c. Send a card that says, "appreciated your visit with us and invite you to join us again" or "enjoyed visiting with you and hope you'll be able to join us."

SENIOR ADULT MISSIONS LEADER

The senior adult missions leader is responsible for locating credible missions opportunities and coordinating class efforts to become involved in missions-related ministry. He or she will also keep abreast of churchwide missions projects and will promote those projects within the class as well.

Ministry Area/Department	Senior adult Sunday School
Position	Senior adult missions leader
Accountable To	Senior adult Bible study teacher
Ministry Target	Senior adults
Position Is	Volunteer
Position May Be Filled By	Church member
Minimum Maturity Level	Stable, maturing Christian
Spiritual Gifts	Exhortation • Serving • Mercy-showing • Giving
Talents or Abilities Desired	Able to research missions opportunities • Discernment
Best Personality Traits	Analyst-dependable • Compassionate • Dedicated
Passion For	Serving the spiritually and physically needy
Length of Service Commitment	One year minimum

ANTICIPATED TIME COMMITMENTS

1. **Doing ministry/preparing for ministry:** one hour a week
2. **Participating in meetings/training:** one hour a month

RESPONSIBILITIES/DUTIES

1. Participate in training opportunities.
2. Work to become informed of ministry needs within congregation, denomination, community and world that would present a missions opportunity for the class.
3. Confirm the credibility of the missions need or project.
4. Inform class of missions opportunities and coordinate missions efforts with class members.
5. Pray for missions opportunities to open and for God's blessing on the missions efforts in which you become involved.
6. Initiate follow-up contacts, when appropriate, with church or community members served through your missions efforts.
7. Involve senior adult outreach leader and church outreach director when needed.
8. Educate class regarding churchwide missions projects and promote the missions theme.

SENIOR ADULT PASTOR

The senior adult pastor will direct and oversee the seniors ministry, minister to senior adult members and follow up with senior adult guests. The senior adult pastor must have a heart for seniors ministry and be willing to work to include this valuable group of people in the ministry of the church.

Ministry Area/Department	Senior adults
Position	Senior adult pastor
Accountable To	Pastor
Ministry Target	Senior adults in the church and community
Position Is	Volunteer or paid staff
Position May Be Filled By	Church member
Minimum Maturity Level	Stable, maturing Christian
Spiritual Gifts	Pastor/shepherd • Mercy-showing • Administration
Talents or Abilities Desired	A retired pastor would be great
Best Personality Traits	Expresser-leader • Compassionate • Dependable • Analytical
Passion For	Ministering to senior adults
Length of Service Commitment	Two years minimum

ANTICIPATED TIME COMMITMENTS

1. **Doing ministry/preparing for ministry:** five hours a week
2. **Participating in meetings/training:** one hour a month

RESPONSIBILITIES/DUTIES

1. Give direction to and oversee the seniors ministry.
   a. Identify the needs and interests of seniors within the church and community.
   b. Plan and develop programs for the seniors ministry, making sure they agree with the seniors-ministry purpose statement.
   c. Evaluate existing programs to determine effectiveness.
   d. Identify and provide ministry opportunities for senior adults.
2. Meet monthly with senior adult ministry leaders to pray and to discuss challenges, solutions and praises.
3. Visit with and minister to senior adult members in their homes and when they are hospitalized or move to a nursing home.
4. Participate in outreach ministry to senior adult guests who have visited the church.
5. Lead prayer and devotional messages in appropriate senior adult meetings.
6. Oversee budget and expenditures for the senior adult ministry.

SENIOR ADULT RECORDS CLERK

The senior adult records clerk is responsible for accurately calculating weekly attendance and offering totals for the senior adult department and for delivering offerings and visitor information to the appropriate staff members.

Ministry Area/Department	Senior adult Sunday School
Position	Senior adult records clerk
Accountable To	Senior adult Bible-study teacher
Ministry Target	Senior adults
Position Is	Volunteer
Position May Be Filled By	Church member
Minimum Maturity Level	New, growing Christian
Spiritual Gifts	Administration • Serving
Talents or Abilities Desired	Good organizational skills • Detail oriented • Good math skills
Best Personality Traits	Dependable
Passion For	Organization • Accuracy • Good stewardship
Length of Service Commitment	One year minimum

ANTICIPATED TIME COMMITMENTS

1. **Doing ministry/preparing for ministry:** one hour a week
2. **Participating in meetings/training:** yearly training workshop

RESPONSIBILITIES/DUTIES

1. Participate in training opportunities, yearly or as presented.
2. Tally class attendance records to obtain weekly attendance figures.
3. Calculate and record total of all classes' tithes and offerings.
4. Deliver all tithes and offerings to treasurer, bookkeeper or appropriate person as set forth in church policy.
5. Assemble visitor forms received from classes and deliver them to the church outreach director or other designated person.

Senior Adult Refreshment Coordinator

The senior adult refreshment coordinator is responsible for planning, organizing and overseeing refreshment preparation and service at special senior adult events.

Ministry Area/Department	Senior adults
Position	Senior adult refreshment coordinator
Accountable To	Senior adult activities coordinator
Ministry Target	Senior adults
Position Is	Volunteer
Position May Be Filled By	Church member
Minimum Maturity Level	New, growing Christian
Spiritual Gifts	Pastor/shepherd • Mercy-showing • Administration • Serving
Talents or Abilities Desired	Accessible by telephone • Good organizational skills
Best Personality Traits	Analyst-expresser-leader • Dependable
Passion For	Hospitality
Length of Service Commitment	One year minimum

Anticipated Time Commitments

1. **Doing ministry/preparing for ministry**: two hours a month
2. **Participating in meetings/training**: minimal, as requested

Responsibilities/Duties

1. Plan refreshments for special activities as needed.
2. Recruit assistants to help prepare or provide refreshments and disposable utensils.
3. Oversee refreshment service setup and cleanup.

SINGLES

COLLEGE HOUSEPARENT/ADOPTIVE FAMILY

The college houseparent or adoptive family will provide encouragement and a sense of family to a local college student or students who have no relatives nearby.

Ministry Area/Department	Singles
Position	College houseparent/adoptive family
Accountable To	College ministries director
Ministry Target	Single adults in college
Position Is	Volunteer
Position May Be Filled By	Church member
Minimum Maturity Level	Stable, maturing Christian
Spiritual Gifts	Pastor/shepherd • Mercy-showing
Talents or Abilities Desired	No criminal background • Good role model • Possess an understanding of the challenges and special needs of college students
Best Personality Traits	Dependable-expresser • Patient • Compassionate
Passion For	Ministering to college students
Length of Service Commitment	One year minimum

ANTICIPATED TIME COMMITMENTS

1. **Doing ministry/preparing for ministry:** four hours a week
2. **Participating in meetings/training:** yearly

RESPONSIBILITIES/DUTIES

1. Provide prayer and emotional support for your adopted college student or students.
2. Touch base with the student(s) weekly and invite them to stop by your home for a visit. Provide homemade cookies or other special treats.
3. Include the student(s) in some family activities and meals.
4. Recognize birthdays, special accomplishments, etc. with cards, celebrations, inexpensive gifts or some type of acknowledgment.

COLLEGE MINISTRIES DIRECTOR

The college ministries director will minister to local college students and include them in the ministry of the church.

Ministry Area/Department	Singles
Position	College ministries director
Accountable To	Singles pastor
Ministry Target	Single adults in college
Position Is	Volunteer
Position May Be Filled By	Church member
Minimum Maturity Level	Stable, maturing Christian
Spiritual Gifts	Pastor/shepherd • Administration
Talents or Abilities Desired	Good organizational skills • Knowledge and understanding of special needs of college students • Education and experience in counseling
Best Personality Traits	Expresser-leader
Passion For	Ministering to college students
Length of Service Commitment	One year minimum

ANTICIPATED TIME COMMITMENTS

1. **Doing ministry/preparing for ministry:** four to six hours a week
2. **Participating in meetings/training:** one hour a month

RESPONSIBILITIES/DUTIES

1. Provide counseling, guidance, prayer and support to local college students.
2. Lead a weekly evening devotional and fellowship time for college students.
3. Arrange for after-church get-togethers at restaurants or homes for the purpose of bonding.
4. Recruit church members to serve as houseparents or adoptive families for college students who are away from home with no family nearby. They should provide encouragement, prayer support and include the student(s) in some family activities and meals.
5. Seek to include college students in the overall ministry of the church.
6. Pray daily for the students, for wisdom in ministering to them and for the strength to be a good role model.
7. Be a good role model, living above reproach, spending time in personal spiritual development and ministry and showing the love of Christ in all you do
8. Be aware of singles activities, college and career-class studies and get-togethers and other church events that could involve the college students. Remain involved as much as possible.
9. Oversee budget and expenditures for the college ministry.

DIVORCE CARE LEADER

The divorce care leader will lead a support group to teach and minister to people who are experiencing or have experienced divorce.

Ministry Area/Department	Singles
Position	Divorce care leader
Accountable To	Singles pastor
Ministry Target	Divorcees
Position Is	Volunteer
Position May Be Filled By	Church member
Minimum Maturity Level	Stable, maturing Christian
Spiritual Gifts	Pastor/shepherd • Teach
Talents or Abilities Desired	Knowledge and understanding of special needs of people who are divorced or are going through divorce • Education or experience in counseling
Best Personality Traits	Dependable-expresser or expresser-leader
Passion For	Ministering to people who are experiencing divorce and helping them rebuild their lives
Length of Service Commitment	One year minimum

ANTICIPATED TIME COMMITMENTS

1. **Doing ministry/preparing for ministry**: two to three hours a week
2. **Participating in meetings/training**: one hour a month

RESPONSIBILITIES/DUTIES

1. Provide spiritual counsel, prayer and support to divorce care participants.
2. Lead a weekly divorce-care group offering spiritual and emotional support in addition to Bible studies on issues of concern to divorced people.
3. Nurture and develop your own spiritual life to gain wisdom and spiritual nourishment for ministry and to provide a positive example to others.

SINGLE ADULT BIBLE STUDY ASSISTANT

The single adult Bible study assistant is the right arm of the single adult Bible-study teacher. The assistant must be prepared to fill in for the teacher when necessary, assist with keeping watch over the flock and coordinating class leaders and functions. The assistant is expected to teach, reach and minister to members and prospects under the direction of the teacher.

Ministry Area/Department	Single adult Sunday School
Position	Single adult Bible study teacher
Accountable To	Sunday School director
Ministry Target	Single adults
Position Is	Volunteer
Position May Be Filled By	Church member
Minimum Maturity Level	Stable, maturing Christian
Spiritual Gifts	Shepherd • Teaching • Exhortation
Talents or Abilities Desired	Communicates well with others • Comfortable speaking in front of a group • Able to allow someone else to lead, but willing to take the lead when necessary • Identifies with special needs of single adults
Best Personality Traits	Dependable-leader • Expresser
Passion For	Discipling single adults
Length of Service Commitment	One year minimum

ANTICIPATED TIME COMMITMENTS

1. **Doing ministry/preparing for ministry**: one to three hours a week
2. **Participating in meetings/training**: one hour a month

RESPONSIBILITIES/DUTIES

1. Develop own relationship with God through Bible study and prayer.
2. Participate in teacher meetings and training opportunities.
3. Study weekly lessons and be available to lead the class in the single adult Bible study teacher's absence.
4. Pray for class members and visitors.
5. Promote spiritual growth and unity among class members.

SINGLE ADULT BIBLE STUDY TEACHER

The single adult Bible study teacher is the shepherd of the class and is responsible for overseeing or coordinating all class leaders and functions. The teacher is expected to teach, reach and minister to members and prospects with the help of other leaders within the class.

Ministry Area/Department	Single adult Sunday School
Position	Single adult Bible study assistant
Accountable To	Single adult Bible study teacher
Ministry Target	Single adults
Position Is	Volunteer
Position May Be Filled By	Church member
Minimum Maturity Level	Stable, maturing Christian
Spiritual Gifts	Shepherd • Teaching • Exhortation
Talents or Abilities Desired	Communicates well with others • Comfortable speaking in front of a group • Able to allow someone else to lead, but willing to take the lead when necessary • Identifies with special needs of single adults
Best Personality Traits	Dependable-leader
Passion For	Discipling single adults and providing support for other leaders
Length of Service Commitment	One year minimum

ANTICIPATED TIME COMMITMENTS

1. **Doing ministry/preparing for ministry:** three hours a week
2. **Participating in meetings/training:** one hour a month

RESPONSIBILITIES/DUTIES

1. Participate in teacher meetings and training opportunities.
2. Work with Sunday School director to choose curriculum for the class.
3. Study and prepare for weekly lessons.
4. Pray for class members and visitors.
5. Arrive 15 minutes before class begins to make sure classroom is prepared and to greet people as they arrive.
6. Lead each week's class and involve participants in studying and learning God's Word through various teaching methods.
7. Promote spiritual growth and unity among class members.
8. Organize class into care groups of six people or less, with one leader per group.

SINGLE ADULT CARE GROUP LEADER

The singles care group leader is responsible for showing Christian love and concern to a small group of single adults through maintaining regular contact and encouragement.

Ministry Area/Department	Single adults
Position	Single adult care group leader
Accountable To	Single adult teacher
Ministry Target	Single adults
Position Is	Volunteer
Position May Be Filled By	Church member
Minimum Maturity Level	New, growing Christian
Spiritual Gifts	Pastor/shepherd • Mercy-showing • Exhortation
Talents or Abilities Desired	A concern for others • Accessible by telephone • Ability to write and mail brief notes and cards
Best Personality Traits	Dependable-expresser-analyst • Compassionate
Passion For	Spiritual and physical well-being of fellow Christians
Length of Service Commitment	One year minimum

ANTICIPATED TIME COMMITMENTS

1. **Doing ministry/preparing for ministry:** one hour a week
2. **Participating in meetings/training:** as requested

RESPONSIBILITIES/DUTIES

Responsible for caring for a small group of singles.

a. Pray for the people in your care group.

b. Send cards when appropriate: birthday, get well, sympathy, etc.

c. Call periodically to touch base with each person in your care group.

d. Call to check on anyone who is absent to let them know they were missed and to make sure everything is all right.

e. With person's permission, pass on any special prayer requests to singles class prayer leader, singles pastor and appropriate class teacher.

f. Notify proper authorities if one of your care-group members has an emergency or critical need for assistance.

SINGLES ACTIVITIES COORDINATOR

The singles activities coordinator will plan and organize regular activities for single adults for the purpose of fun, fellowship and spiritual edification.

Ministry Area/Department	Singles
Position	Singles activities coordinator
Accountable To	Singles pastor
Ministry Target	Single adults
Position Is	Volunteer
Position May Be Filled By	Church member
Minimum Maturity Level	New, growing Christian
Spiritual Gifts	Administration • Exhortation
Talents or Abilities Desired	Good physical health • Planning and organizational skills
Best Personality Traits	Leader-dependable
Passion For	Planning activities for fun, fellowship and spiritual edification of single adults
Length of Service Commitment	One year minimum

ANTICIPATED TIME COMMITMENTS

1. **Doing ministry/preparing for ministry:** one to three hours a week
2. **Participating in meetings/training:** one hour a month

RESPONSIBILITIES/DUTIES

1. Get to know the single adults in the church and find out what their interests are and what activities they enjoy. Do a yearly survey regarding activity choices.
2. Plan and organize monthly activities for all singles.
3. Coordinate special activities with the singles class fellowship leader for specific classes or groups of singles, including
   a. Single-again groups for widows/widowers, divorcees;
   b. Single parents;
   c. Never-marrieds/college and career.
4. Prepare an activity calendar and distribute copies to all singles.
5. Give a copy of the activity schedule to the administrative secretary for when someone calls with questions about dates and activities and so that the information may be included in the church master calendar.

SINGLES CLASS FELLOWSHIP LEADER

The singles class fellowship leader is responsible for planning and coordinating all class social events at church or elsewhere and for recruiting class members to help as needed. This leader will promote unity among the group.

Ministry Area/Department	Single adult Sunday School
Position	Singles class fellowship leader
Accountable To	Single adult Bible study teacher
Ministry Target	Single adults
Position Is	Volunteer
Position May Be Filled By	Church member
Minimum Maturity Level	New, growing Christian
Spiritual Gifts	Administration • Serving • Exhortation
Talents or Abilities Desired	Ability to organize events and motivate people
Best Personality Traits	Expresser-dependable • Sociable
Passion For	Building relationships and encouraging others
Length of Service Commitment	One year minimum

ANTICIPATED TIME COMMITMENTS

1. **Doing ministry/preparing for ministry**: one to two hours a month
2. **Participating in meetings/training**: as requested

RESPONSIBILITIES/DUTIES

1. Develop own relationship with God through Bible study and prayer.
2. Participate in training opportunities.
3. Plan, coordinate and lead class social events; coordinate with singles activities coordinator.
4. Encourage get-acquainted or icebreaker activities within the class.
5. Plan for occasional (or weekly) refreshments before class.

SINGLES CLASS OUTREACH LEADER

The singles class outreach leader is the reaching arm of the class. This person is responsible for contacting and beginning relationships with prospects, visitors and new members in order to point them to Christ and assimilate them into the church through the Sunday School or other Bible study groups.

Ministry Area/Department	Single adult Sunday School
Position	Singles class outreach leader
Accountable To	Single adult Bible study teacher
Ministry Target	Single adults
Position Is	Volunteer
Position May Be Filled By	Church member
Minimum Maturity Level	Stable, maturing Christian
Spiritual Gifts	Exhortation • Evangelism • Administration
Talents or Abilities Desired	Communicates well with others • Organized
Best Personality Traits	Expresser-Leader • Outgoing
Passion For	Influencing single adults for Christ and encouraging them to become involved in the local church
Length of Service Commitment	One year minimum

ANTICIPATED TIME COMMITMENTS

1. **Doing ministry/preparing for ministry:** one hour a week
2. **Participating in meetings/training:** one hour a month

RESPONSIBILITIES/DUTIES

1. Participate in training opportunities.
2. Coordinate efforts with church singles outreach director and inform him or her of visitation progress.
3. Work with class members to identify, witness to and minister to prospects and enroll new members.
4. Develop a class prospect file and keep a record of contacts and the results with those prospects.
5. Pray for prospects, visitors and new members.
6. Initiate follow-up contacts with class visitors by telephone, letter or visit.
7. Contact prospects by telephone, letter or visit to inform them of your class studies, activities, etc. and invite them to participate.
8. Be prepared to lead prospects to Christ or to provide a counselor when needed.
9. Welcome visitors and help new members feel accepted. Introduce them to others and assimilate them into the life of the church.

SINGLES CLASS PRAYER LEADER

The singles class prayer leader is responsible for praying fervently, organizing and leading a class prayer chain and encouraging spiritual growth in class members through daily devotions and prayer.

Ministry Area/Department	Single adult Sunday School
Position	Singles class prayer leader
Accountable To	Single adult Bible study teacher
Ministry Target	Single adults
Position Is	Volunteer
Position May Be Filled By	Church member
Minimum Maturity Level	Stable, maturing Christian
Spiritual Gifts	Exhortation • Mercy-showing • Pastor/shepherd
Talents or Abilities Desired	Communicates well with others • Good listener • Willing to spend time in prayer
Best Personality Traits	Expresser-analyst • Caring • Serious • Discreet
Passion For	Interceding for others in prayer • Belief in the power of prayer
Length of Service Commitment	One year minimum

ANTICIPATED TIME COMMITMENTS

1. **Doing ministry/preparing for ministry**: three hours a week
2. **Participating in meetings/training**: one hour a week (prayer meeting)

RESPONSIBILITIES/DUTIES

1. Develop own relationship with God through Bible study and prayer.
2. Pray daily for the needs of members, prospects and church-related activities and ministries and for church leaders.
3. Organize a class prayer chain through the care group leaders to inform class members of special or urgent prayer needs.
4. Encourage class members to pray for foreign and home missions.
5. Provide or recommend devotional material and exhort members to have daily devotions.

SINGLES CLASS SECRETARY

The singles class secretary is responsible for keeping accurate, up-to-date records; seeing that appropriate forms are completed regarding enrollment changes, visitors, etc.; preparing or assisting with class correspondence when needed; and welcoming newcomers to the class.

Ministry Area/Department	Single adult Sunday School
Position	Singles class secretary
Accountable To	Single adult Bible study teacher
Ministry Target	Single adults
Position Is	Volunteer
Position May Be Filled By	Church member
Minimum Maturity Level	New, growing Christian
Spiritual Gifts	Administration • Serving
Talents or Abilities Desired	Organized • Detail oriented • Good penmanship
Best Personality Traits	Dependable-analyst • Friendly
Passion For	Organization • Accuracy • Serving as a support person
Length of Service Commitment	One year minimum

ANTICIPATED TIME COMMITMENTS

1. **Doing ministry/preparing for ministry**: one hour a week
2. **Participating in meetings/training**: yearly training workshop

RESPONSIBILITIES/DUTIES

1. Develop own relationship with God through Bible study and prayer.
2. Participate in training opportunities yearly, or as presented.
3. Keep accurate records of member attendance and up-to-date personal information—address, phone, birthday, etc.
4. Welcome visitors and help new members feel accepted.
5. Ask visitors to complete appropriate forms or personally register them in your class by obtaining name, address and phone number and determine whether or not they are members of another church.
6. Keep records of visitor and prospect information for outreach purposes. Have this information readily available to the singles Bible study teacher, singles class outreach leader and other concerned staff.
7. Complete weekly attendance form and collect class offerings. Turn them both in to the singles records clerk.
8. Prepare or assist with special correspondence to class members.

SINGLES GUEST FOLLOW-UP ASSISTANT

The singles guest follow-up assistant will follow up every guest who visits the class. This involves making phone calls and visits and writing cards to make the guests feel welcome and cared for.

Ministry Area/Department	Single adults Sunday School
Position	Singles guest follow-up assistant
Accountable To	Singles outreach director
Ministry Target	Single adult church guests
Position Is	Volunteer
Position May Be Filled By	Church member
Minimum Maturity Level	New, growing Christian
Spiritual Gifts	Mercy-showing • Pastor/shepherd
Talents or Abilities Desired	Accessible by telephone • Means of transportation • Ability to write and mail brief notes and cards
Best Personality Traits	Dependable-analyst • Friendly • Compassionate
Passion For	Influencing people for Christ and the church
Length of Service Commitment	One year minimum

ANTICIPATED TIME COMMITMENTS

1. **Doing ministry/preparing for ministry**: one hour a week
2. **Participating in meetings/training**: minimal, as requested

RESPONSIBILITIES/DUTIES

1. Contact all single adult guests who have attended your class.
2. Extend a warm welcome, a hand of fellowship, a note of appreciation or encouragement with the goal of helping the guest feel welcome and influencing him or her to visit again and become committed to Christ and the church.
   a. Phone within 24 hours of visiting class, service or activity. Ask if it's all right to schedule a brief visit.
   b. Visit guest within a week if guest approved or requested a visit. Plan to keep the visit brief, unless the guest asks you to stay longer. Always have someone else visit with you. *Do not go alone.*
   c. Send a card saying "appreciated your visit with us and welcome you to join us again" or "enjoyed visiting with you and hope you'll be able to join us."

SINGLES MISSIONS LEADER

The singles missions leader is responsible for locating credible missions opportunities and coordinating class efforts to become involved in missions-related ministry. He or she will also keep abreast of churchwide missions projects and will promote those projects within the class as well.

Ministry Area/Department	Single adult Sunday School
Position	Singles missions leader
Accountable To	Single adult Bible study teacher
Ministry Target	Single adults
Position Is	Volunteer
Position May Be Filled By	Church member
Minimum Maturity Level	Stable, maturing Christian
Spiritual Gifts	Exhortation • Serving • Mercy-showing • Giving
Talents or Abilities Desired	Ability to research missions opportunities • Discernment
Best Personality Traits	Analyst-dependable • Compassionate • Dedicated
Passion For	Helping the spiritually and physically needy
Length of Service Commitment	One year minimum

ANTICIPATED TIME COMMITMENTS

1. **Doing ministry/preparing for ministry:** one hour a week
2. **Participating in meetings/training:** one hour a quarter

RESPONSIBILITIES/DUTIES

1. Participate in training opportunities.
2. Become informed of ministry needs within congregation, denomination, community and world that present a missions opportunity for the class. You may especially want to look for local opportunities that involve unchurched singles.
3. Do your best to confirm the credibility of the missions need or project.
4. Inform class of missions opportunities and coordinate missions efforts with class members.
5. Pray for missions opportunities and for God's blessing on the missions efforts in which you become involved.
6. When appropriate, initiate follow-up contacts with church or community members served through the class missions efforts.
7. Involve singles outreach leader and church outreach director when needed.
8. Educate class regarding churchwide missions projects and promote the missions theme.

SINGLES OUTREACH LEADER

The singles outreach leader is responsible for identifying outreach opportunities, developing the singles outreach ministry and participating in evangelistic outreach to singles.

Ministry Area/Department	Singles
Position	Singles outreach leader
Accountable To	Church outreach director
Ministry Target	Single adults
Position Is	Volunteer
Position May Be Filled By	Church member
Minimum Maturity Level	Stable, maturing Christian
Spiritual Gifts	Exhortation • Evangelism • Administration
Talents or Abilities Desired	Communicates well with others • Good organizational skills
Best Personality Traits	Expresser-leader • Outgoing
Passion For	Influencing single adults for Christ and encouraging them to become involved in the local church
Length of Service Commitment	One year minimum

ANTICIPATED TIME COMMITMENTS

1. **Doing ministry/preparing for ministry:** one to two hours a week
2. **Participating in meetings/training:** one hour a month

RESPONSIBILITIES/DUTIES

1. Participate in training opportunities.
2. Coordinate efforts with church outreach director to visit single adults.
3. Work with singles class outreach leaders to identify and witness to prospects.
4. Work with singles activities director to plan two to four special activities a year to which single members could invite nonmember singles for the purpose of building relationships and influencing people for Christ.
5. Follow up on visitors who seem receptive or who requested more information or a visit.
6. Pray for prospects, visitors and new members.
7. Be prepared to lead prospects to Christ.

SINGLES PASTOR

The singles pastor will direct and oversee the singles ministry; educate, minister to and include single adult members in the ministry of the church and follow up with single adult guests.

Ministry Area/Department	Single adults
Position	Singles pastor
Accountable To	Pastor
Ministry Target	Single adults
Position Is	Paid staff
Position May Be Filled By	Church member
Minimum Maturity Level	Stable, mature Christian
Spiritual Gifts	Pastor/shepherd • Mercy-showing • Administration
Talents or Abilities Desired	Education and experience in counseling and theology
Best Personality Traits	Expresser-leader • Compassionate • Dependable • Analytical
Passion For	Singles ministry and an understanding of the special needs of single adults
Length of Service Commitment	Two years minimum

ANTICIPATED TIME COMMITMENTS

1. **Doing ministry/preparing for ministry:** eight to ten hours a week
2. **Participating in meetings/training:** one hour a month

RESPONSIBILITIES/DUTIES

1. Give direction to and oversee the singles ministry.
   a. Identify the needs and interests of singles within the church and community.
   b. Plan and develop programs for the singles ministry.
   c. Evaluate existing programs to determine effectiveness.
   d. Identify and provide ministry opportunities for single adults.
2. Meet monthly with singles ministry leaders to pray and to discuss challenges, solutions and praises.
3. Provide counseling and spiritual direction to single adults on an individual basis.
4. Participate in outreach ministry to single adult guests who have visited the church.
5. Lead prayer and devotional messages in appropriate single adult meetings.
6. Plan at least one yearly singles retreat for the purpose of spiritual edification.
7. Arrange special seminars to address specific needs of singles.
8. Visit single adult members who are hospitalized.

9. Participate in training opportunities yearly, or as presented.
10. Oversee budget and expenditures for the singles ministry.

SINGLES RECORDS CLERK

The singles records clerk is responsible for accurately calculating weekly attendance and offering totals for the department and for delivering offerings and visitor information to the appropriate staff members.

Ministry Area/Department	Single adult Sunday School
Position	Singles records clerk
Accountable To	Singles adult Bible study teacher
Ministry Target	Single adults
Position Is	Volunteer
Position May Be Filled By	Church member
Minimum Maturity Level	New, growing Christian
Spiritual Gifts	Administration • Serving
Talents or Abilities Desired	Good organizational skills • Detail oriented • Good math skills
Best Personality Traits	Dependable
Passion For	Organization • Accuracy • Good stewardship
Length of Service Commitment	One year minimum

ANTICIPATED TIME COMMITMENTS

1. **Doing ministry/preparing for ministry:** one hour a week
2. **Participating in meetings/training:** yearly training workshop

RESPONSIBILITIES/DUTIES

1. Develop own relationship with God through Bible study and prayer.
2. Participate in training opportunities, yearly or as presented.
3. Tally class attendance records to obtain weekly attendance figures.
4. Calculate and record total of all classes' tithes and offerings.
5. Deliver all tithes and offerings to treasurer, bookkeeper or other appropriate person as set forth in church policy.
6. Assemble visitor forms received from classes and deliver them to the church outreach director or other designated person.

SINGLES REFRESHMENT COORDINATOR

The singles refreshment coordinator is responsible for planning, organizing and overseeing refreshment preparation and service at special singles events.

Ministry Area/Department	Single adults
Position	Singles refreshment coordinator
Accountable To	Singles activities coordinator
Ministry Target	Single adults
Position Is	Volunteer
Position May Be Filled By	Church member
Minimum Maturity Level	New, growing Christian
Spiritual Gifts	Mercy-showing • Pastor/shepherd • Administration • Serving
Talents or Abilities Desired	Accessible by telephone • Good organizational skills planning and overseeing food service
Best Personality Traits	Analyst-expresser • Dependable
Passion For	Hospitality
Length of Service Commitment	One year minimum

ANTICIPATED TIME COMMITMENTS

1. **Doing ministry/preparing for ministry:** two hours a month
2. **Participating in meetings/training:** minimal, as requested

RESPONSIBILITIES/DUTIES

1. Plan refreshments for special activities as needed.
2. Recruit assistants to help prepare or provide refreshments and disposable utensils.
3. Oversee refreshment service setup and cleanup.

WIDOWS/WIDOWERS SUPPORT GROUP LEADER

The widows/widowers support group leader will lead a support group to encourage, support and educate people who have lost a spouse to death.

Ministry Area/Department	Singles
Position	Widows/widowers support group leader
Accountable To	Singles pastor
Ministry Target	Widows and widowers
Position Is	Volunteer
Position May Be Filled By	Church member
Minimum Maturity Level	Stable, maturing Christian
Spiritual Gifts	Pastor/shepherd • Mercy-showing • Teaching
Talents or Abilities Desired	Education or experience in counseling • Knowledge and understanding of special needs of people who have lost a spouse
Best Personality Traits	Dependable-expresser or expresser-leader
Passion For	Ministering to people who have lost a spouse and helping them meet the challenges they face
Length of Service Commitment	One year minimum

ANTICIPATED TIME COMMITMENTS

1. **Doing ministry/preparing for ministry:** two to three hours a week
2. **Participating in meetings/training:** one hour a month

RESPONSIBILITIES/DUTIES

1. Provide spiritual counsel, prayer and support to widows and widowers of all ages.
2. Lead a weekly support group offering spiritual and emotional support, devotional messages, discussion of concerns and fellowship. May incorporate biblically based studies on issues of concern to widows and widowers.
3. Plan special seminars or courses addressing areas of concern and need, such as handling finances. Some of these seminars might also apply to divorcees and may be held as joint efforts for both single-again groups.
4. Consider inviting community members who are not church members to participate in the support group—a great opportunity to share the love of Christ and draw people to Him.
5. Research and develop a list of dependable people who can provide services such as financial planning, car and home repairs—preferably someone within the church or whom church members can highly recommend.
6. Develop your own spiritual life to gain wisdom and spiritual nourishment for ministry and to provide a positive example to others.

SPORTS

ADULT COACH

The adult coach will oversee and coach a particular sports team in which he or she is skilled. This is an opportunity for fellowship, exercise and outreach; therefore, Christlike attitude and behavior are very important.

Ministry Area/Department	Sports
Position	Adult coach
Accountable To	Executive pastor or activities director
Ministry Target	Adults
Position Is	Volunteer
Position May Be Filled By	Church member
Minimum Maturity Level	New, growing Christian
Spiritual Gifts	Administration • Pastor/shepherd
Talents or Abilities Desired	Skilled in the particular sport to be coached • Sufficient time for coaching
Best Personality Traits	Analyst-expresser or expresser-leader
Passion For	Teaching, motivating and encouraging team members
Length of Service Commitment	One year minimum

ANTICIPATED TIME COMMITMENTS

1. **Doing ministry/preparing for ministry**: two to four hours a week during season
2. **Participating in meetings/training**: yearly

RESPONSIBILITIES/DUTIES

1. Announce team formation and post sign-up sheet.
2. Develop a practice schedule.
3. Schedule an organizational team meeting and inform team members of the meeting. Discuss team name, expectations, equipment needs, proper attire/uniforms, practice schedule, etc.
4. Supervise and coach all practices.
5. Model and encourage a Christlike attitude and behavior.
6. Schedule games with other church or community teams, post game schedule, inform team members and administrative secretary (for church calendar).
7. Praise team for accomplishments and good attitudes.
8. Lead the team in prayer before every practice and game.

ADULT COACH ASSISTANT

The adult coach assistant will assist as needed in coaching a particular sports team in which he or she is skilled. This is an opportunity for fellowship, exercise and outreach; therefore, Christlike attitude and behavior are very important.

Ministry Area/Department	Sports
Position	Adult coach assistant
Accountable To	Adult coach
Ministry Target	Adults
Position Is	Volunteer
Position May Be Filled By	Church member
Minimum Maturity Level	New, growing Christian
Spiritual Gifts	Administration • Pastor/shepherd
Talents or Abilities Desired	Skilled in the particular sport to be coached • Sufficient time for coaching
Best Personality Traits	Analyst-expresser or expresser-leader
Passion For	Teaching, motivating and encouraging team members • Providing leadership support
Length of Service Commitment	One year minimum

ANTICIPATED TIME COMMITMENTS

1. **Doing ministry/preparing for ministry:** two to four hours a week during season
2. **Participating in meetings/training:** yearly

RESPONSIBILITIES/DUTIES

1. Assist coach with development of practice and game schedules.
2. Participate in organizational team meeting.
3. Be familiar with the coach's responsibilities and fill in for coach in case of illness or emergency which prevents him or her from attending a practice or game.
4. Model and encourage a Christlike attitude and behavior.
5. Praise team for accomplishments and good attitudes.
6. Pray before every practice and game.
7. Keep a copy of the team roster with phone numbers. Assist coach with calls in case of change in practice or game schedules.

CHILDREN'S COACH

The children's coach will oversee and coach a particular sports team in which he or she is skilled. This is an opportunity for fellowship, exercise, character building and outreach; therefore, Christlike attitude and behavior are very important.

Ministry Area/Department	Sports
Position	Children's coach
Accountable To	Executive pastor or activities director
Ministry Target	Children
Position Is	Volunteer
Position May Be Filled By	Church member
Minimum Maturity Level	New, growing Christian
Spiritual Gifts	Administration • Pastor/shepherd
Talents or Abilities Desired	Enjoys working with children • Good role model • Skilled in the particular sport to be coached • Sufficient time for coaching • No criminal record
Best Personality Traits	Analyst-expresser or expresser-leader • Patient
Passion For	Teaching, motivating and encouraging team members
Length of Service Commitment	One year minimum

ANTICIPATED TIME COMMITMENTS

1. **Doing ministry/preparing for ministry**: two to four hours a week during season
2. **Participating in meetings/training**: yearly

RESPONSIBILITIES/DUTIES

1. Announce team formation and post sign-up sheet. Determine whether or not to open team membership to neighborhood children.
2. Develop a practice schedule.
3. Schedule an organizational team meeting and inform team members and parents or guardians of the meeting. Discuss team name, expectations, equipment needs, proper attire/uniforms, practice schedule, etc.
4. Supervise and coach at all practices.
5. Model and encourage Christlike attitude and behavior.
6. Schedule games with other church or community teams, post game schedule, inform team members and parents or guardians and give schedule to administrative secretary (for church calendar).
7. Praise team for accomplishments and good attitudes.
8. Lead the team in prayer before every practice and game.

CHILDREN'S COACH ASSISTANT

The children's coach assistant will assist as needed in coaching a particular sports team in which he/she is skilled. This is an opportunity for fellowship, exercise, character building and outreach; therefore, Christlike attitude and behavior are very important.

Ministry Area/Department	Sports
Position	Children's coach assistant
Accountable To	Children's coach
Ministry Target	Children
Position Is	Volunteer
Position May Be Filled By	Church member
Minimum Maturity Level	New, growing Christian
Spiritual Gifts	Administration • Pastor/shepherd
Talents or Abilities Desired	Enjoys working with children • Good role model • Skilled in the particular sport to be coached • Sufficient time for coaching • No criminal record
Best Personality Traits	Analyst-expresser or expresser-leader
Passion For	Teaching, motivating and encouraging team members • Providing leadership support
Length of Service Commitment	One year minimum

ANTICIPATED TIME COMMITMENTS

1. **Doing ministry/preparing for ministry:** two to four hours a week during season
2. **Participating in meetings/training:** yearly

RESPONSIBILITIES/DUTIES

1. Assist coach with development of practice and game schedules.
2. Participate in organizational team meeting.
3. Be familiar with the coach's responsibilities and fill in for coach in case of illness or emergency which prevents him or her from attending a practice or game.
4. Model and encourage a Christlike attitude and behavior.
5. Praise team for accomplishments and good attitudes.
6. Pray before every practice and game.
7. Keep a copy of the team roster with phone numbers. Assist the coach with calls in case of change in practice or game schedules.

Sports First-Aid Volunteer

The sports first aid volunteer is responsible for providing first aid for injuries to church sports team members and for contacting emergency medical care when needed.

Ministry Area/Department	Sports
Position	Sports first-aid volunteer
Accountable To	Coach
Ministry Target	Sports-team players
Position Is	Volunteer
Position May Be Filled By	Church member
Minimum Maturity Level	New, growing Christian
Spiritual Gifts	Serving • Mercy-showing • Pastor/shepherd
Talents or Abilities Desired	Knowledge of administering first aid for sports injuries • Training and experience in first aid or medical field essential • Current CPR certificate
Best Personality Traits	Dependable-analyst
Passion For	Taking care of injuries and comforting the injured
Length of Service Commitment	One year minimum

Anticipated Time Commitments

1. **Doing ministry/preparing for ministry:** two to four hours a week
2. **Participating in meetings/training:** as requested

Responsibilities/Duties

1. Obtain or put together a first-aid kit with appropriate supplies for possible injuries at the game: cold packs, bandages, adhesive bandages, peroxide, antibiotic ointment, etc.
2. Take a first-aid course before serving in this position if there is no previous training in administering first aid. Research current first-aid applications for sports injuries.
3. Attend all sports practices and games; if on a rotating schedule with other first-aid volunteers, make sure you cover your shift.
4. Administer minor first aid as needed.
5. Contact emergency medical help if necessary. Do not attempt to move person if neck injury is suspected. Take care not to do something doubtful that would risk causing further injury. (In other words, know what you're doing or don't do it.)

SPORTS REFRESHMENT COORDINATOR

The sports refreshment coordinator is responsible for recruiting and organizing volunteers to provide refreshments for sports teams after practices and games and for providing water during the games.

Ministry Area/Department	Sports
Position	Sports refreshment coordinator
Accountable To	Coaches/assistant coaches
Ministry Target	Sports-team players
Position Is	Volunteer
Position May Be Filled By	Other approved individual
Minimum Maturity Level	New, growing Christian
Spiritual Gifts	Serving • Exhortation • Administration
Talents or Abilities Desired	Organizational skills • Willing to call to recruit volunteers to donate refreshments for practices and games
Best Personality Traits	Expresser-dependable
Passion For	Serving others
Length of Service Commitment	One year minimum

ANTICIPATED TIME COMMITMENTS

1. **Doing ministry/preparing for ministry:** two to four hours a week during season
2. **Participating in meetings/training:** as requested

RESPONSIBILITIES/DUTIES

1. Obtain roster of players with phone numbers.
2. Contact adult team members and parents or guardians of children's team members to recruit and schedule volunteers to donate soft drinks, lemonade and snacks for after practices and games.
3. Distribute a schedule of refreshment volunteers and dates to each team member.
4. Call to remind volunteers when they are scheduled to provide refreshments.
5. Ensure that team members have ample supply of water during games.

YOUTH COACH

The youth coach will oversee and coach a particular sports team in which he or she is skilled. This is an opportunity for fellowship, exercise, character building and outreach; therefore, Christlike attitude and behavior are very important.

Ministry Area/Department	Sports
Position	Youth coach
Accountable To	Executive pastor or activities director
Ministry Target	Teens
Position Is	Volunteer
Position May Be Filled By	Church member
Minimum Maturity Level	New, growing Christian
Spiritual Gifts	Administration • Pastor/shepherd
Talents or Abilities Desired	Enjoy working with teens • Good role model • Skilled in the particular sport to be coached • Sufficient time for coaching • No criminal record
Best Personality Traits	Analyst-expresser or expresser-leader • Patient
Passion For	Teaching, motivating and encouraging team members
Length of Service Commitment	One year minimum

ANTICIPATED TIME COMMITMENTS

1. **Doing ministry/preparing for ministry:** two to four hours a week during season
2. **Participating in meetings/training:** yearly

RESPONSIBILITIES/DUTIES

1. Announce team formation and post sign-up sheet. Determine whether or not to open team membership to neighborhood teens.
2. Develop a practice schedule.
3. Schedule an organizational team meeting and inform team members and parents or guardians of the meeting. Discuss team name, expectations, equipment needs, proper attire/uniforms, practice schedule, etc.
4. Supervise and coach at all practices.
5. Model and encourage a Christlike attitude and behavior.
6. Schedule games with other church or community teams, post game schedule, inform team members and parents or guardians. Give schedule to administrative secretary (for church calendar).
7. Praise team for accomplishments and good attitudes.
8. Lead the team in prayer before every practice and game.

YOUTH COACH ASSISTANT

The youth coach assistant will assist as needed in coaching a particular sports team in which he or she is skilled. This is an opportunity for fellowship, exercise, character building and outreach; therefore, Christlike attitude and behavior are very important.

Ministry Area/Department	Sports
Position	Youth coach assistant
Accountable To	Youth coach
Ministry Target	Teens
Position Is	Volunteer
Position May Be Filled By	Church member
Minimum Maturity Level	New, growing Christian
Spiritual Gifts	Administration • Pastor/shepherd
Talents or Abilities Desired	Enjoy working with teens • Good role model • Skilled in the particular sport to be coached • Sufficient time for coaching • No criminal record
Best Personality Traits	Analyst-expresser or expresser-leader • Patient
Passion For	Teaching, motivating and encouraging team members • Providing leadership support
Length of Service Commitment	One year minimum

ANTICIPATED TIME COMMITMENTS

1. **Doing ministry/preparing for ministry:** two to four hours a week during season
2. **Participating in meetings/training:** yearly

RESPONSIBILITIES/DUTIES

1. Assist coach with development of practice and game schedules.
2. Participate in organizational team meeting.
3. Be familiar with the coach's responsibilities and fill in for coach in case of illness or emergency which prevents him or her from attending a practice or game.
4. Model and encourage a Christlike attitude and behavior.
5. Praise team for accomplishments and good attitudes.
6. Pray before every practice and game.
7. Keep a copy of the team roster with phone numbers. Assist coach with calls in case of change in practice or game schedules.

STEWARDSHIP

FINANCIAL SECRETARY/BOOKKEEPER

The financial secretary/bookkeeper is responsible for keeping the church's general ledger and financial records and will prepare related forms and reports as necessary, in addition to preparing all checks for the treasurer to sign. This person will help ensure that the church's finances are in accord with legal, ethical and biblical standards.

Ministry Area/Department	Stewardship
Position	Financial secretary/bookkeeper
Accountable To	Executive pastor
Ministry Target	Church in general
Position Is	Paid staff
Position May Be Filled By	Other approved individual
Minimum Maturity Level	New, growing Christian
Spiritual Gifts	Administration • Giving
Talents or Abilities Desired	Some accounting education and background • Good with figures • Discreet • Excellent organizational skills
Best Personality Traits	Dependable-analyst • Detail oriented
Passion For	Good stewardship • Accuracy
Length of Service Commitment	Indefinite

ANTICIPATED TIME COMMITMENTS

1. **Doing ministry/preparing for ministry:** twenty hours a week
2. **Participating in meetings/training:** one hour a month or as needed

RESPONSIBILITIES/DUTIES

1. Keep accurate records of member contributions and prepare year-end summaries for each member for tax and individual review purposes.
2. Keep accurate records of all church income through tithes, offerings and special gifts, and compare to budget estimates.
3. Keep accurate records of all church expenditures and compare to budget allowances.
4. Inform executive pastor if expenditures exceed budget allowances.
5. Prepare financial reports for the executive pastor and church business meetings.
6. Prepare any required reports or forms for the auditor, IRS or other offices of accountability.
7. Be available at church business meetings to answer any questions related to church finances.

8. Prepare weekly payroll checks and related tax records/payments.
9. Prepare checks for monthly church expenses and obligations.
10. Prepare checks for contributions to missions work and other special endeavors.
11. Prepare reimbursement checks upon approval of treasurer.
12. Reconcile and balance church checking accounts.
13. Prepare and distribute W-2 and 1099 forms at the end of the year.

OFFERING COUNTER

The offering counter is responsible for accurately counting the money received in tithes and offerings immediately following collection of the tithes and offerings.

Ministry Area/Department	Stewardship
Position	Offering counter
Accountable To	Treasurer or financial secretary/bookkeeper
Ministry Target	Church in general
Position Is	Volunteer
Position May Be Filled By	Church member
Minimum Maturity Level	New, growing Christian
Spiritual Gifts	Administration • Giving
Talents or Abilities Desired	Accurate counting/math skills
Best Personality Traits	Honest • Trustworthy • Dependable-analyst
Passion For	Good stewardship
Length of Service Commitment	One year minimum

ANTICIPATED TIME COMMITMENTS

1. **Doing ministry/preparing for ministry:** one hour a week
2. **Participating in meetings/training:** one hour initially or as needed

RESPONSIBILITIES/DUTIES

1. Work with at least one other offering counter to carefully count and total offerings after each collection.
2. Write down offering figures for the treasurer and/or financial secretary.
3. Give offerings and offering envelopes to the stewardship clerk.

STEWARDSHIP CLERK

The stewardship clerk will provide clerical assistance to the stewardship director and financial secretary/bookkeeper as needed for special projects or campaigns during the year and will oversee and assist offering counters.

Ministry Area/Department	Stewardship
Position	Stewardship clerk
Accountable To	Treasurer, financial secretary/bookkeeper or stewardship director
Ministry Target	Church
Position Is	Volunteer
Position May Be Filled By	Church member
Minimum Maturity Level	New, growing Christian
Spiritual Gifts	Administration • Serving
Talents or Abilities Desired	Good organizational and math skills • Basic clerical skills • Detail oriented • Willingness to serve and assist others
Best Personality Traits	Honest • Dependable-analyst
Passion For	Good stewardship
Length of Service Commitment	One year minimum

ANTICIPATED TIME COMMITMENTS

1. **Doing ministry/preparing for ministry**: one hour a week (more when planning special projects and campaigns)
2. **Participating in meetings/training**: minimal, as requested

RESPONSIBILITIES/DUTIES

1. Assist with preparing and distributing offering envelopes.
2. Assist stewardship director in preparing for and implementing stewardship campaigns and ongoing stewardship programs.
3. Assist financial secretary/bookkeeper with clerical duties as needed during special projects or extra busy times of the year.
4. Assist and oversee offering counters and turn in offerings and offering totals to the treasurer or financial secretary/bookkeeper after each service where offerings are received.

STEWARDSHIP DIRECTOR

The stewardship director helps provide accountability in the church through leading the development of the church's yearly budget and overseeing budget compliance and by helping evaluate requests for financial aid—benevolence and missions. The stewardship director will also promote an emphasis on good stewardship through planning and implementing yearly stewardship campaigns and ongoing stewardship education.

Ministry Area/Department	Stewardship
Position	Stewardship director
Accountable To	Treasurer, pastor or executive pastor
Ministry Target	Church
Position Is	Volunteer
Position May Be Filled By	Church member
Minimum Maturity Level	Stable, mature Christian
Spiritual Gifts	Administration • Giving
Talents or Abilities Desired	Good organizational skills • Experience in financial planning, accounting or banking fields
Best Personality Traits	Dependable • Analyst-expresser
Passion For	Good stewardship
Length of Service Commitment	Two years minimum

ANTICIPATED TIME COMMITMENTS

1. **Doing ministry/preparing for ministry:** one to two hours a week—possibly more when planning special campaigns
2. **Participating in meetings/training:** one hour a month

RESPONSIBILITIES/DUTIES

1. Lead in developing, overseeing and examining the church's yearly budget.
2. Work with the financial secretary/bookkeeper to track the budget for the various church ministries, touching base with all ministry heads quarterly and at other times if expenditures are exceeding budgeted amount.
3. Meet with benevolence committee to evaluate requests for assistance from benevolence funds.
4. Meet with missions director to evaluate recommendations for missions to support.
5. Plan and implement annual stewardship campaign and/or direct an ongoing stewardship emphasis, working with the pastor. This involves evaluating various options and reviewing campaigns and materials available from sources such as other churches, publishers, denominational headquarters, etc.

TREASURER

The treasurer will help ensure ethical handling of all church funds and oversee management of church banking accounts.

Ministry Area/Department	Stewardship
Position	Treasurer
Accountable To	Pastor or executive pastor (and finance committee)
Ministry Target	Church
Position Is	Volunteer
Position May Be Filled By	Church member
Minimum Maturity Level	Stable, mature Christian
Spiritual Gifts	Administration • Giving
Talents or Abilities Desired	Experience and/or education in the financial field
Best Personality Traits	Trustworthy • Honest • Sincere • Analyst-expresser or analyst-dependable
Passion For	Good stewardship
Length of Service Commitment	Three to five years

ANTICIPATED TIME COMMITMENTS

1. **Doing ministry/preparing for ministry**: one to two hours a week
2. **Participating in meetings/training**: one hour a month or as needed

RESPONSIBILITIES/DUTIES

1. Approve all disbursements.
2. Sign all checks drawn on church bank accounts.
3. Oversee management of church banking accounts.
4. Review monthly statements after reconciliation by financial secretary/bookkeeper.
5. Coordinate and schedule annual audit with an independent audit company.
6. Ensure payment of all missionary support and all financial obligations.
7. Serve on stewardship committee.

TRUSTEE

The trustees will help ensure ethical handling of all church funds and property.

Ministry Area/Department	Stewardship
Position	Trustee
Accountable To	Pastor or executive pastor (and finance committee)
Ministry Target	Church
Position Is	Volunteer
Position May Be Filled By	Church member
Minimum Maturity Level	Stable, mature Christian
Spiritual Gifts	Administration • Giving • Serving
Talents or Abilities Desired	Experience and/or education in business and finance
Best Personality Traits	Trustworthy • Honest • Sincere • Discreet • Levelheaded • Mature • Analyst-expresser or analyst-dependable
Passion For	Good stewardship
Length of Service Commitment	Three to five years

ANTICIPATED TIME COMMITMENTS

1. **Doing ministry/preparing for ministry**: one to two hours a month
2. **Participating in meetings/training**: one to two hours a month or as needed

RESPONSIBILITIES/DUTIES

1. Establish and review procedures for the church's financial management.
2. Serve as legal custodians of all church property.
3. Represent the church in legal matters.
4. Give input/financial advice to the stewardship committee and pastoral staff as requested.
5. Execute bank notes, deeds and other legal documents after receiving approval at the church's business meetings.
6. Examine quarterly financial reports to monitor financial expenditures of the church.
7. Fulfill the laws of this state while serving as a trustee of the church.
8. Assist in the process of awarding contracts for work that must be done to improve or repair church buildings and property.

WOMEN

MOTHERS' MERCY GIVER

The mothers' mercy giver will work with a team of mothers' mercy givers to provide assistance to mothers of babies and young children in times of urgent need. This ministry position may be easiest for women who do not hold a full-time job outside the home.

Ministry Area/Department	Women
Position	Mothers' mercy giver
Accountable To	Women's ministry director
Ministry Target	Mothers of babies and young children
Position Is	Volunteer
Position May Be Filled By	Church member
Minimum Maturity Level	New, growing Christian
Spiritual Gifts	Mercy-showing • Pastor/shepherd
Talents or Abilities Desired	Loves children • Has own transportation • Able to prepare simple meals
Best Personality Traits	Dependable-expresser • Patient
Passion For	Giving moms a break!
Length of Service Commitment	One year minimum

ANTICIPATED TIME COMMITMENTS

1. **Doing ministry/preparing for ministry:** up to four hours a week
2. **Participating in meetings/training:** yearly training or as requested

RESPONSIBILITIES/DUTIES

1. Provide child care in emergency situations.
2. Provide child care while moms go to appointments—doctor, dentist, etc.—if they cannot make other child-care arrangements.
3. Provide transportation to appointments, school, the store and for important errands when car is out of commission.
4. Help prepare or deliver meals when a mother is ill.
5. Do laundry and basic household chores when a mother is recuperating from surgery or childbirth.
6. Pick up and deliver medicine/groceries to sick moms.

Mothers' Prayer Circle Coordinator

The mothers' prayer circle coordinator is responsible for organizing and overseeing the mothers' prayer circle.

Ministry Area/Department	Women
Position	Mothers' prayer circle coordinator
Accountable To	Women's ministry director
Ministry Target	Mothers • Children • Families
Position Is	Volunteer
Position May Be Filled By	Church member
Minimum Maturity Level	New, growing Christian
Spiritual Gifts	Administration • Exhortation • Pastor/shepherd
Talents or Abilities Desired	Organizational skills • Belief in the power of prayer
Best Personality Traits	Dependable-leader • Expresser
Passion For	Uplifting mothers and sharing their concerns in prayer
Length of Service Commitment	One year minimum

Anticipated Time Commitments

1. Doing ministry/preparing for ministry: two hours a week
2. Participating in meetings/training: one hour a month

Responsibilities/Duties

1. Enlist members in the mothers' prayer circle.
2. Organize and coordinate the mothers' prayer circle.
3. Prepare a list of women who want to be involved in an emergency prayer chain by phone. Include names and phone numbers. Distribute the list and explain the procedure to participants.
4. Meet with mothers on a weekly basis to pray for their families and children; children in the church, community and local schools—and for parents and leaders in the church, community and local schools.
5. Pray daily for special prayer requests from women in the mothers' prayer circle.
6. Become a spiritual prayer warrior, remembering the emotional, physical and spiritual needs of children—especially the need for protection from evil influences in today's world.

MOTHERS' PRAYER CIRCLE MEMBER

The mothers' prayer circle member is responsible for participating in the mothers' prayer circle as a prayer warrior for children in the church, community and local schools as well as for special prayer requests from mothers within the circle.

Ministry Area/Department	Women
Position	Mothers' prayer circle member
Accountable To	Mothers' prayer circle coordinator
Ministry Target	Mothers, children and families
Position Is	Volunteer
Position May Be Filled By	Church member
Minimum Maturity Level	New, growing Christian
Spiritual Gifts	Pastor/shepherd • Mercy-showing
Talents or Abilities Desired	Belief in the power of prayer
Best Personality Traits	Any and all
Passion For	Spiritual nurture and safety of children
Length of Service Commitment	Indefinite

ANTICIPATED TIME COMMITMENTS

1. **Doing ministry/preparing for ministry:** one to two hours a week
2. **Participating in meetings/training:** as requested

RESPONSIBILITIES/DUTIES

1. Consider participating in an emergency prayer chain for mothers.
2. Meet with mothers' prayer circle on a weekly basis to pray for their families and children, children in the church, community and local schools—and parents and leaders in the church, community and local schools.
3. Pray daily for special prayer requests from women in the mothers' prayer circle.
4. Become a spiritual prayer warrior, remembering the emotional, physical and spiritual needs of children—especially the need for protection from evil influence in today's world.

SHOWER ASSISTANT

The shower assistant is responsible for helping the shower hostess plan and carry out showers for the women in the church who are expecting a baby or getting married.

Ministry Area/Department	Women
Position	Shower assistant
Accountable To	Shower hostess
Ministry Target	Brides and mothers-to-be
Position Is	Volunteer
Position May Be Filled By	Church member
Minimum Maturity Level	New, growing Christian
Spiritual Gifts	Serving • Pastor/shepherd • Administration
Talents or Abilities Desired	Good organizational skills • Enjoys planning and serving
Best Personality Traits	Analyst-dependable or dependable-expresser
Passion For	Honoring and helping others during special occasions
Length of Service Commitment	One year minimum

ANTICIPATED TIME COMMITMENTS

1. **Doing ministry/preparing for ministry:** three to five hours the week of the shower
2. **Participating in meetings/training:** as requested

RESPONSIBILITIES/DUTIES

1. Meet with the shower hostess to plan and prepare for the shower.
    a. Help prepare and mail invitations, make phone calls and place announcements in church publications.
    b. Help determine type and amount of refreshments needed. Contact volunteers to bring refreshments.
    c. Assist shower hostess with errands to purchase supplies/refreshments.
    e. If games are planned, help plan them and purchase inexpensive gifts.
2. Help set up for the shower, serve during the shower and clean up afterward.

SHOWER HOSTESS

The shower hostess is responsible for planning a special celebration to honor and shower with gifts the women in the church who are expecting a baby or getting married.

Ministry Area/Department	Women
Position	Shower hostess
Accountable To	Women's ministry director
Ministry Target	Brides and mothers-to-be
Position Is	Volunteer
Position May Be Filled By	Church member
Minimum Maturity Level	New, growing Christian
Spiritual Gifts	Serving • Pastor/shepherd • Administration
Talents or Abilities Desired	Good organizational skills for planning and organizing showers
Best Personality Traits	Leader-analyst or leader-dependable
Passion For	Honoring and helping others during special occasions
Length of Service Commitment	One year minimum

ANTICIPATED TIME COMMITMENTS

1. **Doing ministry/preparing for ministry:** three to five hours the week of the shower
2. **Participating in meetings/training:** as requested

RESPONSIBILITIES/DUTIES

1. Maintain a shower fund from regular donations from church members—most likely from women. Use this fund for paper/plastic goods, inexpensive gifts for game prizes, invitations and refreshments—or ask volunteers to donate these items.
2. Maintain a supply of reusable decorations for showers.
3. Schedule a shower for women of the church who are expecting a child or getting married. Check the church master calendar and with the individual for whom the shower will be given to confirm a date that does not conflict with other activities.
4. Meet with shower assistants to plan and prepare for the shower. Contact other committees or recruit volunteers to assist as needed.
   a. Prepare and mail invitations and place an announcement in the church newsletter inviting church members; include an RSVP so you can have an idea of the number of people attending in order to plan appropriately.
   b. Determine type and amount of refreshments needed. Purchase and/or assign volunteers to bring refreshments.

      c. Purchase disposable plates, utensils, cups, napkins.

      d. Plan games and purchase inexpensive gifts (if you decide to include games).

5. Plan prayer and a brief devotional or Scripture reading related to the upcoming event.

6. Set up for and oversee the shower and clean up afterward with the help of assistants.

WEDDING CONSULTANT

The wedding consultant is responsible for providing advice and assistance to the bride in planning her wedding and for conducting the rehearsal and wedding as planned and according to church policies.

Ministry Area/Department	Women
Position	Wedding consultant
Accountable To	Women's ministry director
Ministry Target	Brides
Position Is	Paid staff—paid per wedding by the bride and groom
Position May Be Filled By	Church member
Minimum Maturity Level	New, growing Christian
Spiritual Gifts	Serving • Administration
Talents or Abilities Desired	Very good organizational skills • Creative • Knowledge of wedding etiquette and church policies regarding weddings • Able to direct groups • Clean, well-dressed appearance
Best Personality Traits	Expresser-leader • Analyst
Passion For	Working with brides to plan and conduct memorable weddings
Length of Service Commitment	Two years minimum

ANTICIPATED TIME COMMITMENTS

1. **Doing ministry/preparing for ministry:** depending on need—may be zero hours some months and several hours other months
2. **Participating in meetings/training:** minimal, as requested

RESPONSIBILITIES/DUTIES

1. Meet with the bride and probably the bride's mother to discuss bride's and groom's wishes and give your suggestions and insight.
2. Develop an order of service. Type and print out copies for yourself, the pastor officiating the wedding and the wedding party.
3. If bulletins will be used, compile information from the order of service and wedding party information for the bulletins. Print out the information for the bride and prepare the bulletins if being paid extra to do so.
4. Plan and conduct the wedding rehearsal.
5. Direct the wedding and reception if being held at the church.

WOMEN'S ACTIVITIES COORDINATOR

The women's activities coordinator is responsible for planning and coordinating activities for women of the church to promote fellowship and spiritual growth and to address special needs of women.

Ministry Area/Department	Women
Position	Women's activities coordinator
Accountable To	Women's ministry director
Ministry Target	Women
Position Is	Volunteer
Position May Be Filled By	Church member
Minimum Maturity Level	Stable, maturing Christian
Spiritual Gifts	Pastor/shepherd • Administration • Teaching
Talents or Abilities Desired	Good planning and organizational skills
Best Personality Traits	Leader-analyst • Dependable
Passion For	Promoting a sense of unity by bringing women together
Length of Service Commitment	One year minimum

ANTICIPATED TIME COMMITMENTS

1. **Doing ministry/preparing for ministry:** three hours a month
2. **Participating in meetings/training:** one hour a month

RESPONSIBILITIES/DUTIES

1. Plan special activities for women at least every other month. Activities may include, but are not limited to
   a. Educational/health-related classes on women's issues;
   b. Biblically based classes on women's roles;
   c. Craft and home fix-it workshops;
   d. Saturday breakfast out;
   e. Prayer retreat at a member's lakefront or mountain cabin; and
   f. Tea party with testimonies and prayer.
2. Work with women's ministry director to plan and coordinate a yearly trip to hear a special inspirational women's speaker. Or attend a women's event sponsored by a denomination, a nearby Christian college, a university or church.

WOMEN'S DAY OUT COORDINATOR

The women's day out coordinator is responsible for planning and coordinating activities for women of the church to provide a time out or refreshing break from the everyday responsibilities women face.

Ministry Area/Department	Women
Position	Women's day out coordinator
Accountable To	Women's ministry director
Ministry Target	Women, especially stay-at-home moms
Position Is	Volunteer
Position May Be Filled By	Church member
Minimum Maturity Level	New, growing Christian
Spiritual Gifts	Pastor/shepherd • Administration
Talents or Abilities Desired	Good planning and organizational skills
Best Personality Traits	Expresser-analyst • Dependable
Passion For	Giving women a break and providing opportunities for fun and fellowship
Length of Service Commitment	One year minimum

ANTICIPATED TIME COMMITMENTS

1. **Doing ministry/preparing for ministry:** four to six hours every other month
2. **Participating in meetings/training:** one hour every other month

RESPONSIBILITIES/DUTIES

1. Plan and oversee special daytime outings for women at least every other month. Activities may include, but are not limited to:
   a. Going on garden tours;
   b. Visiting museums;
   c. Going shopping;
   d. Having lunch and attending an afternoon movie.
2. Plan and oversee special nighttime or Saturday outings at least twice a year to include women who work outside the home. Activities may include, in addition to above:
   a. Attending an evening movie;
   b. Going to a nice restaurant for a relaxing dinner.
3. Arrange babysitting service at the church for women who need such services.

WOMEN'S MINISTRY DIRECTOR

The women's ministry director will provide direction and vision and will organize, coordinate and oversee the women's ministries of this church.

Ministry Area/Department	Women
Position	Women's ministry director
Accountable To	Pastor
Ministry Target	Women
Position Is	Volunteer
Position May Be Filled By	Church member
Minimum Maturity Level	Stable, mature Christian
Spiritual Gifts	Pastor/shepherd • Administration
Talents or Abilities Desired	Able to relate well with other people • Creative • Good organizational skills
Best Personality Traits	Analyst-expresser or expresser-leader • Dependable
Passion For	Ministering to women and providing opportunities for women to minister through the church
Length of Service Commitment	Two years minimum

ANTICIPATED TIME COMMITMENTS

1. **Doing ministry/preparing for ministry:** two to four hours a week
2. **Participating in meetings/training:** one hour a month

RESPONSIBILITIES/DUTIES

1. Meet regularly—perhaps monthly—with the various women's ministry coordinators and directors to discuss progress, praises, challenges, solutions and new ideas.
2. Be available to talk with women's ministry leaders about concerns or needs they may have.
3. Participate in special events and activities for women.
4. Work with the women's activities director to plan a special yearly trip to an inspirational event for women.
5. Read, research and evaluate materials on women's ministries and apply what you learn to this church's women's ministry.
6. Provide training opportunities for women leaders in the church.
7. Pray regularly for the women of the church.
8. Act as a liaison between the women's ministries and the pastor.
9. Develop a women's ministries budget to present to the appropriate committee each year.
10. Oversee the distribution of funds for women's ministries and keep track of budget expenditures.

WOMEN'S MISSIONS COORDINATOR

The women's missions coordinator is responsible for overseeing the women's missions ministry, including exploring missions opportunities, keeping women informed regarding potential and ongoing missions involvement, coordinating efforts and serving as a liaison between the church and missionaries.

Ministry Area/Department	Women
Position	Women's missions coordinator
Accountable To	Women's ministry director
Ministry Target	Women, community and world missions
Position Is	Volunteer
Position May Be Filled By	A church member
Minimum Maturity Level	Stable, mature Christian
Spiritual Gifts	Pastor/shepherd • Exhortation • Administration • Giving • Serving • Evangelism
Talents or Abilities Desired	Organizational and leadership skills • Time to research and verify missions opportunities
Best Personality Traits	Dependable-analyst or expresser-analyst
Passion For	Assisting people in need of spiritual and physical help and sharing the love of God with them
Length of Service Commitment	Two years minimum

ANTICIPATED TIME COMMITMENTS

1. **Doing ministry/preparing for ministry:** two hours a month—more during special emphases
2. **Participating in meetings/training:** one hour a month

RESPONSIBILITIES/DUTIES

1. Act as a liaison with missionaries and organizations that women's ministry supports.
2. Research, locate, validate and follow up on missions projects, opportunities and needs within the local community as well as mission fields. Concentrate on areas of specific interest to women, such as:
   a. Local shelters for abused or homeless women and children;
   b. Christian after-school programs;
   c. Orphanages—local and foreign;
   d. Missions organizations that reach out with physical and spiritual help around the world;
   e. Children who have a parent in jail or prison—coordinate with prison ministry.

3. Organize the women's ministry's efforts in supporting missions.
4. Educate the church regarding the women's ministry missions projects.

WOMEN'S PHYSICAL FITNESS DIRECTOR

The women's physical fitness director is responsible for leading a regular exercise group to help meet women's physical needs and promote healthy living.

Ministry Area/Department	Women
Position	Women's physical fitness director
Accountable To	Women's ministry director
Ministry Target	Women of the church and community
Position Is	Paid staff
Position May Be Filled By	Other approved individual
Minimum Maturity Level	New, growing Christian
Spiritual Gifts	Pastor/shepherd • Exhortation • Serving
Talents or Abilities Desired	Education or experience with women's health issues, physical fitness and nutrition
Best Personality Traits	Expresser-leader
Passion For	Encouraging women to feel their best and take care of themselves
Length of Service Commitment	One year minimum

ANTICIPATED TIME COMMITMENTS

1. **Doing ministry/preparing for ministry:** three to six hours a week
2. **Participating in meetings/training:** as requested

RESPONSIBILITIES/DUTIES

1. Survey the women of the church to determine the need and interest for morning and evening programs. Schedule classes depending on results of survey.
2. Consider setting a nominal fee for the class—$1 per person per class—to help pay for the instructor and supplies. Supplies to consider:
   a. Instructional videos
   b. Tasteful music to exercise by
   c. Scales for checking weight
   d. Pamphlets on women's health issues
   e. Progress/participation charts
3. Lead the fitness groups in exercise, followed by a brief devotional and glass of cold water or juice. Each session should last no longer than one hour.

YOUTH

YOUTH ACTIVITIES ASSISTANT

The youth activities assistant is responsible for providing supervision and assisting the youth activities coordinator as needed during activities that promote fun, fellowship, spiritual development and ministry involvement among teens.

Ministry Area/Department	Youth
Position	Youth activities assistant
Accountable To	Youth activities coordinator
Ministry Target	Teens
Position Is	Volunteer
Position May Be Filled By	Church member
Minimum Maturity Level	New, growing Christian
Spiritual Gifts	Pastor/shepherd • Teaching
Talents or Abilities Desired	Enjoys the challenge of working with teens and understands characteristics of teens • Good role model • No criminal record
Best Personality Traits	Dependable-expresser
Passion For	Providing leadership support and making a positive difference in the lives of teens
Length of Service Commitment	One year minimum

ANTICIPATED TIME COMMITMENTS

1. **Doing ministry/preparing for ministry:** four hours a month
2. **Participating in meetings/training:** one hour a month

RESPONSIBILITIES/DUTIES

1. Participate in and assist with supervising activities for teens—from one to four times a month, depending on number of volunteers. Types of activities include:
   a. Our activities—fun and fellowship for teens who are regularly involved in our youth program;
   b. Outreach activities—fun activities for reaching out to unsaved or unchurched teens, building relationships and presenting the gospel;
   c. Others activities—ministry opportunities for teens to use their spiritual gifts and talents in Christian service.
2. Be familiar with the youth activities calendar.
3. Meet with youth activities coordinator once a month to review the upcoming month's activities and receive training as necessary.

4. Distribute and receive activities permission slips when needed and give them to the youth activities coordinator.

5. Provide encouragement and positive reinforcement to teens.

6. Pray for the teens and activity success prior to each activity.

YOUTH ACTIVITIES COORDINATOR

The youth activities coordinator is responsible for planning, coordinating and overseeing activities for teens to promote fun, fellowship, spiritual development and ministry involvement.

Ministry Area/Department	Youth
Position	Youth activities coordinator
Accountable To	Youth pastor
Ministry Target	Teens
Position Is	Volunteer
Position May Be Filled By	Church member
Minimum Maturity Level	Stable, mature Christian
Spiritual Gifts	Pastor/shepherd • Administration • Teaching
Talents or Abilities Desired	Good planning and organizational skills • Good role model • No criminal record
Best Personality Traits	Leader-analyst • Dependable
Passion For	Organizing activities and promoting a sense of unity and fellowship among teens
Length of Service Commitment	Two years minimum

ANTICIPATED TIME COMMITMENTS

1. **Doing ministry/preparing for ministry**: four to eight hours a month
2. **Participating in meetings/training**: one hour a month

RESPONSIBILITIES/DUTIES

1. Plan special weekly activities for teens. Vary the types of activities from:
   a. Our activities—fun and fellowship for teens who are regularly involved in our youth program;
   b. Outreach activities—fun activities for reaching out to unsaved or unchurched teens, building relationships and presenting the gospel;
   c. Others activities—ministry opportunities for teens to use their spiritual gifts and talents in Christian service.
2. Maintain contact with youth missions coordinator to plan missions activities.
3. Develop and maintain a youth activities calendar. Every youth leader and teen and the administrative secretary should receive a copy of each month's activity calendar.
4. Recruit volunteers to become youth activities assistants to help oversee and carry out weekly activities; rotate volunteers to serve every other week, once a month or with specific types of activities.

5. Meet with youth activities assistants once a month to review the upcoming month's activities and provide training as necessary.

6. Develop/provide travel activities permission slips for parents to complete and sign, containing emergency information; keep these on file and take copies with the group when traveling. Check with church's insurance company regarding a proper liability release statement.

7. Pray for guidance and direction and for great spiritual results from the activities.

YOUTH CARE GROUP LEADER

The youth care group leader is responsible for showing Christian love and concern to a small group of teens through maintaining regular contact and encouragement.

Ministry Area/Department	Youth
Position	Youth care group leader
Accountable To	Youth teacher
Ministry Target	Teens
Position Is	Volunteer
Position May Be Filled By	Church member
Minimum Maturity Level	Stable, maturing Christian
Spiritual Gifts	Pastor/shepherd • Mercy-showing • Exhortation
Talents or Abilities Desired	Concern for others • Accessible by telephone • Able to write and mail brief notes and cards • Good role model • No criminal record
Best Personality Traits	Dependable-expresser-analyst • Compassionate
Passion For	Spiritual and physical well-being of fellow Christians
Length of Service Commitment	One year minimum

ANTICIPATED TIME COMMITMENTS

1. Doing ministry/preparing for ministry: two hours a week
2. Participating in meetings/training: as requested

RESPONSIBILITIES/DUTIES

Responsible for caring for a small group of teens.

a. Pray for the people in your care group.
b. Send cards when appropriate: birthday, thinking of you, get well, sympathy, congratulations, etc.
c. Call periodically to touch base with each person in your care group.
d. Call to check on anyone who is absent to let them know they were missed and to make sure everything is all right.
e. With person's permission, pass on any special prayer requests to youth class prayer leader, youth pastor and appropriate youth teacher.
f. Notify proper minister or authorities if one of your care-group members has an emergency or critical need for assistance.

YOUTH CHAPERONE

The youth chaperone is responsible for supervising teens to ensure safe and orderly activities and trips.

Ministry Area/Department	Youth
Position	Youth chaperone
Accountable To	Youth activities coordinator or youth pastor
Ministry Target	Teens
Position Is	Volunteer
Position May Be Filled By	Church member
Minimum Maturity Level	Stable, maturing Christian
Spiritual Gifts	Serving • Exhortation
Talents or Abilities Desired	Able to communicate well with teens and understand their characteristics and challenges • Good role model • No criminal record
Best Personality Traits	Patient • Consistent • Dependable
Passion For	Providing positive influence and direction for teens
Length of Service Commitment	One year minimum

ANTICIPATED TIME COMMITMENTS

1. **Doing ministry/preparing for ministry**: two to four hours a week
2. **Participating in meetings/training**: yearly workshop or upon request

RESPONSIBILITIES/DUTIES

1. Participate in training opportunities yearly, or as presented.
2. Greet teens before activities.
3. Help keep order in the activities.
4. Help supervise teens during trips and special activities.
5. Ensure that rules and policies are followed. Be familiar with them ahead of time.
6. Deal with disciplinary problems in a discreet manner. Call parents if necessary. Inform youth pastor of any problems.
7. Pray for wisdom before every event, activity or trip.

YOUTH CLASS SECRETARY

The youth class secretary is responsible for keeping accurate, up-to-date records; seeing that appropriate forms are completed regarding enrollment changes and visitors; preparing or assisting with class correspondence when needed and welcoming students to the class.

Ministry Area/Department	Youth
Position	Youth class secretary
Accountable To	Youth teacher
Ministry Target	Teens
Position Is	Volunteer
Position May Be Filled By	Church member
Minimum Maturity Level	New, growing Christian
Spiritual Gifts	Administration • Serving
Talents or Abilities Desired	Good organizational skills • Attention to detail • Good penmanship • Good role model • No criminal record of child abuse
Best Personality Traits	Dependable • Cheerful
Passion For	Encouraging teens
Length of Service Commitment	One year minimum

ANTICIPATED TIME COMMITMENTS

1. **Doing ministry/preparing for ministry:** two hours a week
2. **Participating in meetings/training:** yearly training workshop.

RESPONSIBILITIES/DUTIES

1. Participate in training opportunities yearly, or as presented.
2. Keep accurate records of member attendance and up-to-date personal information—address, phone, birthday, etc.
3. Welcome visitors, help new members feel accepted and greet all attendees.
4. Prepare name tags for class leaders and for visitors as they arrive.
5. Register visitors in your class by obtaining name, address, phone number and determine whether or not they are a member of another church.
6. Keep records of visitor and prospect information for outreach purposes. Have this information readily available to the youth teacher, youth outreach leader or other concerned staff.
7. Complete weekly attendance form, collect class offerings and turn them in to youth records clerk.
8. Prepare or assist with special correspondence to class members.

YOUTH COUNSELOR/MENTOR

The youth counselor/mentor is responsible for providing emotional and spiritual nurturing to one teen and for being a positive role model and influence in that teen's life.

Ministry Area/Department	Youth
Position	Youth counselor/mentor
Accountable To	Youth pastor
Ministry Target	Teens
Position Is	Volunteer
Position May Be Filled By	Church member
Minimum Maturity Level	Stable, maturing Christian
Spiritual Gifts	Pastor/shepherd • Mercy-showing • Exhortation • Teaching
Talents or Abilities Desired	Heartfelt concern for teens • Accessible by telephone • Training or experience in counseling desired, but not required • Student of God's Word • Must understand the maturity levels and characteristics of teens and the challenges they face today • Good role model • No criminal record
Best Personality Traits	Dependable-expresser or expresser-leader
Passion For	Spiritual and physical well-being of teens
Length of Service Commitment	One year minimum

ANTICIPATED TIME COMMITMENTS

1. **Doing ministry/preparing for ministry**: one hour a week (more during times of special need)
2. **Participating in meetings/training**: yearly workshop

RESPONSIBILITIES/DUTIES

1. Provide a good role model for a teen who desires a counselor/mentor.
2. Be available for phone calls from the teen throughout the week. Sharpen your listening skills!
3. Plan times to get together with your teen for ice cream or lunch and a chat or some simple activity to show that you care.
4. Regularly pray for and with your teen.
5. Share life experiences and lessons.
6. When asked for advice, provide it based on biblical principles and wisdom gained from experience.
7. Send cards when appropriate: birthday, get well, sympathy, congratulations, etc.

YOUTH FUND-RAISING COORDINATOR

The youth fund-raising coordinator is responsible for planning, coordinating and overseeing activities to raise funds for youth ministry needs.

Ministry Area/Department	Youth
Position	Youth fund-raising coordinator
Accountable To	Youth pastor
Ministry Target	Teens
Position Is	Volunteer
Position May Be Filled By	Church member
Minimum Maturity Level	New, growing Christian
Spiritual Gifts	Giving • Exhortation
Talents or Abilities Desired	Creative thinker • Able to plan and coordinate fund-raising activities • Good role model • No criminal record
Best Personality Traits	Analyst-expresser or leader-analyst
Passion For	Raising funds in support of youth ministry
Length of Service Commitment	One year minimum

ANTICIPATED TIME COMMITMENTS

1. **Doing ministry/preparing for ministry:** four to eight hours a quarter
2. **Participating in meetings/training:** one hour a quarter

RESPONSIBILITIES/DUTIES

1. Research and develop fund-raising activities.
2. Plan and direct quarterly fund-raising activities that include teens' participation.
3. Provide sign-up sheets and recruit teens and teens' relatives when necessary to participate in fund-raising activities.
4. Ensure that sufficient supervision is provided at fund-raising events and activities, using youth chaperones/parents.
5. Oversee collection and handling of funds. Turn in funds to financial secretary for deposit in youth ministry budget; note if for special purpose such as a missions trip or for general budget.

YOUTH GUEST FOLLOW-UP ASSISTANT

The youth guest follow-up assistant will follow-up every teenage guest who visits a youth class or activity. This involves phone calls, visits and cards to make the guests feel welcome and cared for.

Ministry Area/Department	Youth
Position	Youth guest follow-up assistant
Accountable To	Youth outreach director
Ministry Target	Teen guests
Position Is	Volunteer
Position May Be Filled By	Church member
Minimum Maturity Level	New, growing Christian
Spiritual Gifts	Mercy-showing • Pastor/shepherd • Evangelism
Talents or Abilities Desired	Accessible by telephone • Means of transportation • Able to write and mail brief notes and cards • Good role model • No criminal record
Best Personality Traits	Dependable-analyst • Friendly • Compassionate
Passion For	Influencing people for Christ and the church
Length of Service Commitment	One year minimum

ANTICIPATED TIME COMMITMENTS

1. **Doing ministry/preparing for ministry:** two to four hours a week
2. **Participating in meetings/training:** minimal, as requested

RESPONSIBILITIES/DUTIES

1. Contact all teenage guests who have attended a youth class or activity.
2. Extend a warm welcome, a hand of fellowship, a note of appreciation or encouragement with the goal of helping the guest feel welcome and influencing him or her to visit again and become committed to Christ and the church.
   a. Phone within 24 hours of visiting class, service or activity. Ask if all right to schedule a brief visit.
   b. Visit guests within a week after request or approval. Plan to keep the visit brief, unless the guest asks you to stay longer. Always have someone else visit with you—perhaps someone with the gift of evangelism. *Do not go alone.* Plan to tell about the church and youth ministry and upcoming activities. Be prepared to pray for special requests from the guest and to provide spiritual direction if the opportunity arises.
   c. Send a card saying "appreciated your visit with us and welcome you to join us again" or "enjoyed visiting with you and hope you'll be able to join us."

 The Big Book of Job Descriptions for Ministry

Youth Missions Coordinator

The youth missions coordinator is responsible for locating credible missions opportunities and coordinating youth efforts to become involved in missions ministry. He or she will also keep abreast of churchwide missions projects and will promote those projects within the youth ministry as well.

Ministry Area/Department	Youth
Position	Youth missions coordinator
Accountable To	Youth pastor
Ministry Target	Teens
Position Is	Volunteer
Position May Be Filled By	Church member
Minimum Maturity Level	Stable, maturing Christian
Spiritual Gifts	Exhortation • Serving • Mercy-showing • Giving
Talents or Abilities Desired	Able to research missions opportunities • Discernment • Good role model • No criminal record
Best Personality Traits	Analyst-dependable • Compassionate • Dedicated
Passion For	Helping the spiritually and physically needy
Length of Service Commitment	One year minimum

Anticipated Time Commitments

1. Doing ministry/preparing for ministry: one hour a week
2. Participating in meetings/training: one hour a quarter

Responsibilities/Duties

1. Participate in training opportunities.
2. Become informed about ministry needs within congregation, denomination, community and the world that present a missions opportunity for the youth ministry.
3. Do your best to confirm the credibility of the missions need or project.
4. Inform youth classes of missions opportunities and coordinate missions efforts.
5. Pray for missions opportunities to open and for God's blessing on the missions efforts in which you become involved.
6. When appropriate, initiate follow-up contacts with church or community members served through your missions efforts.
7. Coordinate special missions activities with the youth activities coordinator.
8. Educate your youth classes regarding churchwide missions projects and promote the missions theme.

YOUTH OUTREACH LEADER

The youth outreach leader is responsible for contacting and beginning relationships with prospects, visitors and new members of the youth group in order to point them to Christ and assimilate them into the church through Sunday School or other Bible-study groups.

Ministry Area/Department	Youth
Position	Youth outreach leader
Accountable To	Youth pastor
Ministry Target	Teens
Position Is	Volunteer
Position May Be Filled By	Church member
Minimum Maturity Level	Stable, maturing Christian
Spiritual Gifts	Exhortation • Evangelism • Administration
Talents or Abilities Desired	Able to communicate well with others • Organized • Good role model • No criminal record
Best Personality Traits	Expresser-leader • Outgoing
Passion For	Influencing teens for Christ and encouraging them to become involved in the local church
Length of Service Commitment	One year minimum

ANTICIPATED TIME COMMITMENTS

1. **Doing ministry/preparing for ministry:** two to four hours a week
2. **Participating in meetings/training:** one hour a month

RESPONSIBILITIES/DUTIES

1. Participate in training opportunities.
2. Coordinate efforts with church outreach director and inform of visitation progress.
3. Work with youth class members to identify, witness to and minister to prospects and enroll new members.
4. Develop a prospects file and keep a record of contacts and results.
5. Pray for prospects, visitors and new members.
6. Initiate follow-up contacts with youth class visitors: phone, write, visit.
7. Contact prospects to inform them of youth class studies and activities, and invite them to participate: phone, write, visit.
8. Be prepared to lead prospects to Christ or to provide a counselor when needed.
9. Welcome visitors and help new members feel accepted; introduce them to others; assimilate them into the life of the church.

YOUTH PASTOR

The youth pastor will direct and oversee the youth ministry; educate, minister to and include teens in the ministry of the church and follow up with teen guests.

Ministry Area/Department	Youth
Position	Youth pastor
Accountable To	Pastor
Ministry Target	Teens
Position Is	Paid staff
Position May Be Filled By	Church member
Minimum Maturity Level	Stable, mature Christian
Spiritual Gifts	Pastor/shepherd • Mercy-showing • Administration • Teaching
Talents or Abilities Desired	Education and experience in theology and counseling • Good role model • No criminal record
Best Personality Traits	Expresser-leader • Compassionate • Dependable • Analytical
Passion For	Ministering to and with teens, with a heart for understanding their special needs and a desire to include this valuable group of people in the ministry of the church
Length of Service Commitment	Two years minimum

ANTICIPATED TIME COMMITMENTS

1. **Doing ministry/preparing for ministry:** forty hours a week, off on Saturday and one day during week, except for emergencies and special occasions
2. **Participating in meetings/training:** one hour a month

RESPONSIBILITIES/DUTIES

1. Give direction to and oversee the youth ministry.
   a. Identify the needs and interests of teens within the church and community.
   b. Plan and develop programs for the youth ministry.
   c. Evaluate existing programs to determine effectiveness.
   d. Identify and provide ministry opportunities for teens.
2. Meet monthly with youth ministry leaders to pray and to discuss upcoming events, challenges, solutions and praises.
3. Recruit youth workers as needed. Provide training for youth workers as needed. Plan one major training/inspirational workshop a year.
4. Provide counseling and spiritual direction to teens on an individual basis.
5. Participate in outreach ministry to teens who have visited the church: visits, letters, etc.

6. Lead midweek Bible study for teens.

7. Plan at least one yearly youth retreat for the purpose of spiritual edification.

8. Visit teens who are hospitalized.

9. Participate in training opportunities yearly, or as presented.

10. Develop the youth ministry budget and track expenditures throughout the year.

11. Compile a youth directory, have copies made and distribute to teens and youth workers.

YOUTH RECORDS CLERK

The youth records clerk is responsible for accurately calculating weekly attendance and offering totals for the youth department and for delivering offerings and visitor information to the appropriate staff members.

Ministry Area/Department	Youth Sunday School
Position	Youth records clerk
Accountable To	Youth teacher
Ministry Target	Teens • Youth leaders
Position Is	Volunteer
Position May Be Filled By	Church member
Minimum Maturity Level	New, growing Christian
Spiritual Gifts	Administration • Serving
Talents or Abilities Desired	Good organizational skills • Detail oriented • Good math skills
Best Personality Traits	Dependable-analyst
Passion For	Accuracy • Good stewardship
Length of Service Commitment	One year minimum

ANTICIPATED TIME COMMITMENTS

1. **Doing ministry/preparing for ministry:** one hour a week
2. **Participating in meetings/training:** yearly training workshop

RESPONSIBILITIES/DUTIES

1. Participate in training opportunities yearly, or as presented.
2. Tally class attendance records to obtain weekly attendance figures.
3. Calculate and record total of all classes' tithes and offerings.
4. Deliver all tithes and offerings to treasurer, financial secretary/bookkeeper or appropriate person as set forth in church policy.
5. Assemble visitor forms received from classes and deliver them to the youth outreach director or other designated person.

YOUTH SNACK COORDINATOR

The youth snack coordinator is responsible for planning, organizing and overseeing refreshment preparation and service at special youth events.

Ministry Area/Department	Youth
Position	Youth snack coordinator
Accountable To	Youth activities coordinator
Ministry Target	Teens
Position Is	Volunteer
Position May Be Filled By	Church member
Minimum Maturity Level	New, growing Christian
Spiritual Gifts	Pastor/shepherd • Administration • Serving
Talents or Abilities Desired	Accessible by telephone • Good organizational skills
Best Personality Traits	Analyst-expresser • Dependable
Passion For	Hospitality (planning, organizing and overseeing food service)
Length of Service Commitment	One year minimum

ANTICIPATED TIME COMMITMENTS

1. **Doing ministry/preparing for ministry**: two to eight hours a month
2. **Participating in meetings/training**: minimal, as requested

RESPONSIBILITIES/DUTIES

1. Plan refreshments for special activities as needed.
2. Recruit assistants—contact by phone or in person or post a sign-up sheet—to help prepare or provide refreshments and disposable utensils.
3. Oversee refreshment service setup and cleanup.

YOUTH TEACHER

The youth teacher is the shepherd of the class and is responsible for keeping watch over the flock, providing spiritual nurture through biblical instruction, guidance and positive role modeling.

Ministry Area/Department	Youth Sunday School
Position	Youth teacher
Accountable To	Youth pastor
Ministry Target	Teens
Position Is	Volunteer
Position May Be Filled By	Church member
Minimum Maturity Level	Stable, maturing Christian
Spiritual Gifts	Shepherding • Teaching • Exhortation
Talents or Abilities Desired	Able to communicate well with teens • Knowledge of God's Word • Good role model • No criminal record
Best Personality Traits	Dependable • Compassionate
Passion For	Nurturing, teaching and leading teens to Jesus and a Christian lifestyle
Length of Service Commitment	One year minimum

ANTICIPATED TIME COMMITMENTS

1. **Doing ministry/preparing for ministry:** three hours a week
2. **Participating in meetings/training:** one hour a month

RESPONSIBILITIES/DUTIES

1. Participate in teacher meetings and training opportunities.
2. Work with the Sunday School director and youth pastor to choose study curriculum.
3. Study and prepare for each weekly lesson. Gather necessary materials: handouts, props, supplies, etc.
4. Pray for class members and visitors.
5. Arrive 15 minutes before class begins to make sure classroom is prepared and to greet students as they arrive.
6. Lead each week's class and involve teens in studying and learning God's Word through various teaching methods and activities.
7. Promote spiritual growth and unity among class members.
8. Maintain contact with teens and parents. Keep teens and parents informed of topics/themes being studied, special events, etc. through printed notices, postcards and calls. Call, visit or send cards to students on special occasions or when a student is sick; youth class secretary can assist with these duties.

YOUTH TEACHER ASSISTANT

The youth teacher assistant is the right arm of the youth teacher. The assistant must be prepared to fill in for the teacher when necessary and assist with keeping watch over the flock and coordinating class functions. The assistant is expected to teach, reach and minister to members and prospects under the direction of the teacher.

Ministry Area/Department	Youth Sunday school
Position	Youth teacher assistant
Accountable To	Youth pastor
Ministry Target	Teens
Position Is	Volunteer
Position May Be Filled By	Church member
Minimum Maturity Level	Stable, maturing Christian
Spiritual Gifts	Shepherding • Serving • Exhortation
Talents or Abilities Desired	Able to communicate well with teens • Able to allow someone else to lead, but willing to take the lead when necessary • Knowledge of God's Word • Good role model • No criminal record
Best Personality Traits	Dependable
Passion For	Discipling teens o Providing support for other leaders
Length of Service Commitment	One year minimum

ANTICIPATED TIME COMMITMENTS

1. **Doing ministry/preparing for ministry:** two hours a week
2. **Participating in meetings/training:** one hour a month

RESPONSIBILITIES/DUTIES

1. Participate in teacher meetings and training opportunities.
2. Study each weekly lesson and be available to lead the class in the youth teacher's absence.
3. Assist youth teacher with preparing materials for class: handouts, props, supplies, etc.
4. Distribute handouts or other instructional material in class.
5. Pray for class members and visitors.
6. Promote spiritual growth and unity among class members.
7. Greet and encourage students.

CGI Discovery Tools

Team Ministry Spiritual Gifts Inventory, by Larry Gilbert. With nearly 3 million in use, *Team Ministry Spiritual Gifts Inventory* has helped Christians around the world identify their God-given spiritual gifts. Administered in 20 minutes, it is a fun and valuable tool for the Christian walk. Show your members how God has equipped them to minister in your local church! *Includes questionnaire and carbonless, self-scoring answer sheet with instructions and brief gift descriptions.*

Versions Available:
English Adult - 401S • English Youth - 401Y
Chinese Adult - 401C • Korean Adult - 401K • Spanish Adult - 401X
All versions in 8.5- x 11-inch format

1-9 = $2.50 ea • 10-49 = $2.20 ea
50-99 = $1.65 ea • 100+ = $1.10 ea

God's Special Gifts for Me, by Larry Gilbert. A different approach to teaching spiritual gifts. This fun, lively, illustrated pamphlet uses Bible characters to teach children, ages 8-12, about spiritual gifts and helps them see how they can also serve God through using their special gifts! *Includes brief lessons, questionnaire, and scoring section in one 16-page booklet (5.25- x 8.5-inch).*

1-49 = $2.50 ea • 50-99 = $2.00 ea
100+ = $1.50 ea

Spiritual Growth Survey, by David Slamp. Help Christians identify the progress they are making in their own spiritual journey. When an entire congregation takes this spiritual survey, the pastor can view the results as a planning tool to determine what he needs to teach to help his members strengthen those areas in which they are weak. *Includes questionnaire; carbonless, self-scoring answer sheet; and instructions.*

1-9 = $2.50 ea • 10-49 = $2.20 ea
50-99 = $1.65 ea • 100+ = $1.10 ea

Leadership/Management Inventory, by Larry Gilbert. Every leader and manager has a unique style for leading and managing. This quick, easy-to-use, self-grading inventory will help you and your leaders discover your personal leadership/management styles. *Includes questionnaire with answer sheet and description of each style, giving the pros and cons of each.*

1-9 = $2.50 ea • 10-49 = $2.20 ea
50-99 = $1.65 ea • 100+ = $1.10 ea

Team Decision-Making Inventory, by Glen Martin and Larry Gilbert. This inventory will help you identify how each of your members functions best — whether a Doer, Collector, Planner, or Analyzer. Then you can determine if you need additional help due to a lack of input, skills, or gifts in your own team. *Includes questionnaire; carbonless, self-scoring answer sheet; and instructions.*

1-9 = $2.50 ea • 10-49 = $2.20 ea
50-99 = $1.65 ea • 100+ = $1.10 ea

L•E•A•D Personality Inventory, by Walt Lacey. This inventory will provide you with an in-depth study of the unique characteristics of each type of personality. Your entire church will benefit from gaining a complete knowledge and understanding of their own personalities. Find out what motivates/demotivates them, and how they are most/least effective. *Includes questionnaire, answer sheet, and instructions.*

1-99 = $4.75 ea • 100+ = $3.75 ea

Leadership Effectiveness Inventory, by Walt Lacey. This on-the-job assessment tool identifies specific leadership skills, provides objective assessment of leadership abilities, pinpoints areas in need of development, and establishes a path to improve leadership performance. *Includes 7 inventories for self-assessment, to assess others' leadership skills, or for others to assess your leadership skills.* $43.95

Inventory Sample Pack, contains 7 different inventories! If you're curious to know about our inventories and want to try them yourself before you order for your staff or congregation *or* if you just want inventories for personal use, then you'll want to order this sample pack. *Includes Spiritual Gifts Inventory, Youth Spiritual Gifts Inventory, God's Special Gifts For Me, Leadership/Management Inventory, Team Decision-Making Inventory, L•E•A•D Personality Inventory, and Spiritual Growth Survey. Each includes instructions, questionnaire, and answer sheet.* $9.95

Church Growth Institute: providing practical tools for leadership, evangelism, and church growth –and helping you and your church reach your potential for Christ.

For a FREE online Spiritual Gifts Analysis, go to www.TeamMinistry.com

Visit our website! www.churchgrowth.org

TO ORDER: CALL 1-800-553-GROW (4769)

9:00 a.m. to 8:00 p.m. EST Monday - Friday
Fax: 1-800-860-3109 • E-mail: cgimail@churchgrowth.org • Mail: CGI, P.O. Box 9176, Oxnard, CA 93031

Your Name _____ Phone _____
Church Name _____ FAX _____
Street Address _____
City/State/Zip _____
Your Position in Church _____ E-mail _____
__ Payment Enclosed. __ Bill Church. __ Charge to (circle one): MasterCard VISA DISCOVER AMERICAN EXPRESS
Card #_____ Exp. Date _____

Item #	Description	Price	Qty.	Total
	Shipping and handling			
	TOTAL			

Shipping and Handling
$0.00 - $6.00.....................$2.00
$6.01 - $20.00..................$3.50
$20.01 - $100.00................$6.50
$100.01 and over.................7%
Foreign Orders: Additional Charges Apply

Ephesians Four Ministries
CHURCH GROWTH INSTITUTE
P.O. Box 7, Elkton, MD 21922-0007
Orders: P.O. Box 9176, Oxnard, CA 93031-9176